The Young Professional's Book of Ballet

Angela Whitehill and William Noble

with an introduction by David Howard

A Dance Horizons Book
Princeton Book Company, Publishers
Princeton, NJ

Jamie and Pamela,

to you love always

A Dance Horizons Book
Princeton Book Company, Publishers
POB 57
Pennington, NJ 08534

Cover photograph © Jim William
Cover design by Main Street Design
Book design by Meg Davis
Typeset by Peirce Graphic Services, Inc.

Library of Congress Cataloging-in-Publication Data

Whitehill, Angela.
    The young professional's book of ballet / Angela Whitehill and William Noble with an introduction by David Howard.
      p. cm.
    "A Dance Horizons book."
    Includes bibliographical references.
    ISBN 0-87127-147-8
    1. Ballet—Vocational guidance. 2. Ballet dancers—Employment.
I. Noble, William. II. Title.
GV1787.W47   1990
792.8'023—dc20   90-53352

792.8
Whi

Contents

Introduction

I recall my first performance with the Royal Ballet, a moment I had waited for through so many years of hard work and frustrating progress. Finally, I was going to dance with the company that most English ballet lovers hail with superlatives. I was going to be part of that tradition!

I had joined the company on tour and was cast as a huntsman in the second act of *Swan Lake*. I had no rehearsal, and when I walked into the dressing room to get ready for the performance, I asked where my costume could be found.

No one answered me; the other dancers turned their heads or continued with their costume preparations. It was as if I was invisible.

I waited, hoping someone would speak to me, but there was only silence. I knew, then, that I had but one choice if I wanted to continue dancing. I waited until everyone was costumed and had left the dressing room. There was only one costume remaining, and I put it on.

It was huge and hung like a sack, but I knew it had to be mine. As the newest company member, my choices started at the bottom of the ladder!

Dancers, of course, are extremely territorial, and what supports this is particular company protocol. In the Royal Ballet at that time, new dancers were barely acknowledged and rarely helped by other dancers, until they showed they could make their own way. The territorial nature of all this can be seen in who stands where at the barre, who sits where in the dressing room, who makes up before whom. It preserves a dancer's identity and provides some form of hierarchy.

Matters such as this are what form the backbone of this new book, and the authors have tailored their prose to the practical concerns of the young dancer. But, then, who exactly is the young dancer? Is she—or he—barely into apprenticeship, in the first few weeks of a full company contract, experiencing the rigors of touring, facing the decision to join a foreign company?

The answer is that the young dancer is all of the above, that each step in a career could bring exposure to one or more of these choices. A young dancer remains "young" not because of age but because of experience. What this book does is illuminate such experience so that the young dancer will benefit from it. The experiences of others can be translated into practical advice which will allow a dance career to move along more smoothly and positively.

Ballet training is difficult and confusing, and once the young dancer has graduated from high school and made the decision to follow a career in ballet, questions multiply: What about auditioning, apprenticeships, contracts? How do I deal with my new life?

As a professional, the young dancer is faced with different concerns because that's what a career demands. Take medical benefits, for example. In preprofessional days, there was someone—a parent or school program—to look after these things, to arrange them and to pay for medical attention when there was injury. Now, the young dancer has to fit within a company medical program, and that means paying for medical insurance as well as understanding its limitations. It also means the young professional has to have the maturity to cope with self-responsibility.

Certainly, a fundamental decision for every young professional is finding the right company to join. It takes research, and it is a major step on the path to self-reliance. One might think that the swirl of well-meaning questions and suggestions from friends and relatives could make it all unmanageable, but this book helps sort out what is important and what is not. There is practical advice here that every young dancer should become familiar with because the matter of choosing a company *is* crucial. If a dancer joins the company where he or she has trained, the answers may come more easily, even where the company is separate from the school. But lately I see young dancers choosing smaller companies in regional areas, choosing to settle in less populated towns and cities where life is less hectic. It is a welcome trend because it means that the ballet art will be spread in a wider arc, involving more people and places. For the young professional there will be more opportunity, and for ballet generally there will be greater exposure.

One of the things that I impress upon my students is that ballet is more than stage talent, more than being able to perform four perfect pirouettes or thirty-two fouettés to each side. Ballet is also *back*stage talent, the ability to survive the heated competition among one's peers, the ability to get along in an atmosphere where every dancer has one eye on himself or herself and one eye on everyone else. Learning to do the things that don't create friction and don't create embarrassment (as in my costuming faux pas before my first performance with the Royal Ballet) are as important as executing a proper arabesque or tendu. The dancer's world is much larger than the physical limits of the stage, and this book underscores it. Attending to backstage etiquette, dealing with costumes and shoes, getting along with the nonartistic staff, understanding nonperformance responsibilities are all here, as they should be. As a teacher I urge students to become familiar with these things, and as a former dancer I welcome the advice and the help.

Young dancers today are more realistic about their careers. We've tried to develop such awareness in the hope that expectations can be realized with a minimum of disappointment. When I was dancing professionally, there were few places to turn for practical advice, and we were often left with assumptions and yearnings that never materialized. Now we have books such as this, and I, for one, am delighted because it provides my students with no-nonsense information, and it adds support to the wonderful art of ballet.

—*David Howard, ballet master,*
David Howard Dance Center

On the Verge   1

*Dancing is the loftiest, the most moving, the most
beautiful of the arts, because it is no mere translation or
abstraction, it is life itself.*
—Havelock Ellis, psychologist and author

You've finally made the decision to try the professional ballet
world. Good for you.

How do you get ready? What do you do first? Do you print a
résumé, do you have photographs taken, who should do them, where
should you send them? Are the auditions any different than the ones you
participated in as a student? What should you wear, how should you act?
What do company directors look for?

So many questions. You know most of the answers already; your
training has prepared you for the precise moment. And there are answers
you can find months before the audition season.

Because there are many dancers and few companies, and because funds
are limited, dancers think the process of choice lies only with the artistic
director. But you do have choices if you do your homework.

And if you start eighteen months before you plan to audition.

WHERE DO I FIT IN?

*None of us is suited to dance everywhere, but there will
always be a place for you to dance somewhere.*
—Arthur Leeth, ballet master, Boston Ballet

The first thing you need to do is buy the latest edition of *Stern's Performing
Arts Guide* (from *Dance Magazine*, NYC). It lists all the companies in the
United States, and other parts of North America and in Europe. It's
important to get the latest edition because companies change so often.

Ask yourself: Where would I like to live? Where are my friends dancing? Whose choreography do I admire? What type of dancer am I? Classical? Contemporary? Powerful? Lyrical? Do I want to join a major company or a regional one?

Now, draft a simple letter to the public relations director of the companies that interest you. Ask for a copy of a recent program and any recent reviews and feature articles about the company or company members. (Don't ask for a *Nutcracker* program or souvenir; it won't tell you what you want to know.) Include a large stamped, self-addressed envelope.

From a simple program you can learn a lot:

Is the format like a Playbill? (If it's just a single piece of paper, the company may be small and transient.) Does the company have a subscription series in the same theatre? If so, it is probably well established in the community.

The masthead page will tell you how many dancers are in the company, if they use the star system, if they have an apprentice program (paid and unpaid), if they use an orchestra, and how large the production and design staff is.

The current program will give you an idea of the repertoire. (Also check to see what the company will be dancing in its next series.) Who is being cast in which ballets, do the corps de ballet and apprentices dance the whole repertoire, how much of the repertoire is choreographed by the artistic director?

On the page that lists production staff you can learn still more. Are there production, technical and stage managers, lighting, scenic and costume designers, wardrobe personnel, or are one or two people doing it all? If the latter is true, the budget may be small and you might find yourself helping to load floors and scenery or iron costumes. Occasionally this can be fun, but it is not what you are trained to do or want to do regularly.

You will certainly want to check the dancers' biographies. How long has each dancer been with the company? This is important. Happy dancers, who are being cast regularly and have a chance to advance up the dancer's ladder (see chap. 3), stay in one company. Where were they trained? In the co-affiliated school? In a particular syllabus? Are they from all over the country or the world?

If the dancers come from many areas and schools, then this would be a good place to audition. But even if the dancers are trained in the affiliated school, don't despair. Consider attending that school for a year or joining the summer program for six weeks in your junior year of high school. Artistic directors tend to find this a comfortable way to choose dancers.

"We like to look at our dancers, work with them, get to know a little about them before taking them into the company," says Francia Russel, artistic director of Pacific Northwest Ballet.

"I often choose apprentices when I am teaching in summer workshops," says Robert Barnett of the Atlanta Ballet.

It's remarkable isn't it? The more the artistic directors get to know *you*, the more you'll get to know *them*. It makes the choice that much easier and more reassuring.

Now turn to the back of the program where the list of donors is found. How does the company support itself? Are there corporate, business, and private donors? Is there a Ballet Guild or a Friends of the Ballet Association? Do the community, city, and state give grants? Yes, you should know this information. This is where your salary comes from.

Ballet companies depend on donations, endowments, grants, and fund-raising events for the money to cover the budget. Performance fees and box office receipts aren't enough. You need to be aware of the company's financial status in order to protect yourself and your career.

Lastly, look at the advertisements: Do they reflect an interest in the ballet or are they the generic kind? Does the business community care about dance? If so, chances are the company has good solid support in the community, and you won't find yourself worrying over your next pay check.

Whether you want to join a regional or major metropolitan company is really your preference. You should decide whether you are ready to audition for a company such as American Ballet Theatre, Joffrey, or San Francisco Ballet or whether you need to get some experience in a smaller company where you will have a chance to perform more frequently and get more individual attention.

Ask yourself:

• Are you confident and outgoing?

• Do you love big cities?

• Can you handle pressure?

• Do you love to dance for thousands of people or for hundreds?

• Would you like to tour?

• Are you technically ready for a big company or do you need more training?

In a major company you must be self-sufficient both technically and personally. Life in the big cities can be lonely and frightening.

On arrival in a regional city you will probably be housed with a family, while you find an apartment. You will meet people in the community immediately. In the city you will probably have to live alone in a hostel while finding an apartment.

Most major companies belong to a union which means your salary will be larger, but so will your expenses.

The demands of a major company are not always greater than a regional one. There are more dancers vying for the same parts, but there are more casts for each ballet. On the other hand, this often means less chance to perform.

Individual attention in class may be less in a large company. (In a union company you are not *required* to attend daily company class; many New York dancers choose to take their morning class with private teachers such as David Howard or Mdme Darvash.) In a regional company the artistic director often teaches daily class or rehearsal; he is more likely to cast you in soloist roles, especially during *Nutcracker* season.

Politics and competition abound in every company. They are more complex in a major one, however, and it may take you longer to be promoted to soloist. But you will be dancing with, and can learn from watching, the great stars in the company.

Most companies tour: the major ones internationally, the smaller ones regionally.

Your decisions about your career are no different than those of your (nondancing) peers. Do you want to join a major corporation or a small business?

By now your drawers are overflowing with programs and you've made a list of each company's strengths, so it's time for the next step.

RÉSUMÉ, RÉSUMÉ, RÉSUMÉ

> *When sending a résumé, make it short and meaningful, not something that looks like a mass mailing.*
> —Carolyn Clark, artistic director, New Jersey Ballet

Everyone needs a résumé. It's that part of you which lingers with the artistic director before and after your audition. It is a record of who you are, where you've been, what you've learned, and how much value you will be to the company. Good résumés can help you get a job, and every dancer should maintain one and keep it up to date. See page 131 for a sample résumé.

The format you choose reflects your personality. Don't use elaborate graphics—a simple border or none at all will do. And above all, keep it BRIEF. One page if possible, two at the most.

Your name comes first in bold type or underlined, followed by your permanent address and phone number (include the area code). If you aren't living at home, also add your current address and phone number and the dates you expect to be moving on (résumés often stay in files for years).

Next comes your height, weight, coloring, and age. The director needs this information to determine whether you will fit with the look of the corps de ballet. Be as accurate as you can. Any fudging and it will be uncovered at your audition.

If you have not danced in a professional company (*Nutcracker* doesn't count) then your training comes next, but list only your professional preparation, from the age of ten, regardless of how long you have been with the school. Make sure to include major summer workshops you have attended, again from the age of ten.

Who were your TEACHERS? They come next. Don't forget to include guest and master teachers and, if possible, provide their affiliation: ballet master, Cincinnati Ballet; artistic director, Atlanta Ballet; and so forth.

Head the next section ROLES DANCED and include the name of the company (underlined), followed by the roles you have danced. Principal roles first, followed by soloist, then corps de ballet parts. Do include the name of guest artists if you have been partnered, as well as the role you danced.

Don't include recitals.

If you are also a modern or jazz dancer, list those roles separately, but include the same information: company, role, guest artists who've partnered you.

At the end of your résumé include any major awards, competition, or academic honors, such as the President's Award for Excellence in the Arts, or any major ballet competitions you have won. This section should be titled GRANTS AND AWARDS.

It is easier and less time consuming to put your résumé on a word processor and save it. Then, as events in your life change or your dance orientation changes, you simply punch in the changes and print out a new copy. If you don't have a word processor, any reputable secretarial service can do the job for you.

Choose good quality paper in your favorite color (not *too* bright!) and have the first twenty-five copies run off on a reliable copy machine.

During the time you are working on your résumé, send out another simple letter to the companies that interest you. This letter should go to the artistic directors (their names are listed under the company names in *Stern's Performing Arts Guide*). Ask where and when the next auditions will be held. Sign each letter personally, and include your height because many companies are quite specific about how tall they want their dancers. You don't want to spend time attending an audition only to find you were excluded before you ever walked to the barre.

In your letter you should ask if the company will be needing dancers next season. Most companies can't really answer this question before April or May because they probably haven't wrapped up yearly contract talks, but you never know what might be open. At least the director will know your interest is not casual.

Now don't be surprised if you hear nothing from some—even most—of the companies. It is, unfortunately, the nature of the business that a lack of interest means a lack of attention. Don't take it personally; don't let it deflect you. Keep those letters going out.

And remember: your résumé should contain the following headings:

Name:_____

Address:_____

Phone Number:_____

Height:_____

Weight:_____

Coloring:_____

Age:_____

TRAINING:_____

TEACHERS:_____

ROLES DANCED:_____

GRANTS AND AWARDS:_____

PAMELA E. WHITEHILL

A good composite resumé photograph is of great importance before auditioning for a professional company. © Linda Alaniz, Martha Swope.

YOUR PHOTOGRAPHIC IMAGE

> *Treat a photo call like a performance; photographs last forever.* —Martha Swope, dance photographer

Now is the time to arrange for photographs. Make an appointment with the best photographer you can afford. Make sure he or she is a well-known dance photographer. Check to see if he or she is listed in *Stern's Performing Arts Guide.*

If there is no dance photographer nearby and you can't afford to travel to one in a major city, you will have to do some research. Contact your local arts council for recommendations, speak to other dancers, even get in touch with a local sports photographer (they are used to action). Explain to the sports photographer about turnout, pirouettes, feet, alignment, and épaulement, making sure he or she *really* understands. The studio backdrop must be completely plain, preferably simple photographer's paper. Remember your legs and body will look longer if you are photographed from below. Ask for a full-length mirror in the studio or ask your teacher or a dancer friend to accompany you for technical advice.

Next, be *fully prepared*—know your strongest points. If you jump well, then prepare jumping poses; if you have a great line, know at which angle it looks best.

Never forget . . . show yourself at your best!

For instance, when you choose a costume make sure it flatters you more than any other costume you might pick. The camera will add weight—don't forget that—and always remember to wear a costume that is immaculately clean and well pressed. Keep a travel iron handy, and make sure you've brought your headdresses.

Before you leave for the photographer's studio, do the following:
- Check your makeup bag and make sure you have all you might need. If there's no makeup artist at the studio, you can handle this yourself.

- Get your hair clean and shiny; the first shots may be with your hair down. Don't forget to take hair pins, nets, elastics, gel, and spray.

- Take a class with a teacher you know, someone who makes you feel great! Now, you'll be warm and ready to look your best.

In about a week your photos will arrive in contact-sheet form. Look at them through a magnifying glass, scrutinizing every inch of your body and technique; analyze, analyze!

Now is the time to use all of those things you have learned through the years. You *must* know yourself; you must know what works and what doesn't work. Remember, the director is probably as picky as you are.

Choose the three or four best photos. That's all. The temptation will be to pick many more than you can use, but control yourself. You can always place another order with the photographer.

If you choose a headshot it should be combined with a full-length photo. A photograph of your face only tells the director you are beautiful, not

Although a hometown studio can take excellent photos, they may not be equipped to capture a young dancer. The subject looks short and undramantic, the backdrop and shadows detract from her, and a cotton leotard adds weight to her body. Cynthia Thompson. © Everett Photo Studio.

Taken from above, this photo shortens the dancer's legs and distorts her line. Legs are shown to their best advantage with shots from below. Pamela Whitehill.

This head shot merely shows a director that the dancer looks like a dancer but not whether she can dance. Wendy Fish. © Linda Alaniz, Martha Swope.

Here is a photo that shows the dancer can move and enjoys it. Cynthia Thompson. © Everett Photo Studio.

whether you can dance, but you will need the headshot for the program later.

List the contact-sheet numbers below the photos you choose. Ask for 8″ × 10″ size of the ones you have chosen.

Now make plans to get inexpensive reproductions through one of the major photo services. Look in the "Resource" section of *Stern's Performing Arts Guide*. (Hopkins Photo Service in New York is one of the best. They will make a negative and reproduce it in quantity inexpensively and quickly.) Plan on twenty-five for your first order. The negative is a one-time cost—you return it to them each time you require more photos. (Be careful to store it in its original envelope.)

You must decide whether you want a single photo or a composite of several shots per page, whether you want your name printed on the front of the photo, whether you want your height, weight, coloring, phone and address printed there too. (You will need to send the photo service a layout design.)

Or, if you prefer, you can have your résumé attached to the back of the photo.

There are no hard and fast rules about all of this. It's a matter of personal style and what you think will make you look your best—your photo sells you as a competent, well-trained professional.

A dramatic photo can leave a lasting impression: Two years after Pamela started using the photograph on page 10 she auditioned for a company to which she had sent that photo with her original résumé circulation. The director singled her out at the audition and handed the photo back. Her concern turned to delight when he said, "We have one of these on file already. I know, it's very dramatic, one I always remembered!"

Auditioning for a Job   *2*

> *It doesn't take long to realize that the other dancers are*
> *not watching you but worrying about themselves.*
>   *—Pamela Whitehill, dancer*

*M*any times it begins this way: a simple phone call to the studio, student to teacher: "I'm so excited about auditioning. I went to New York a month ago, I had Martha Swope do my photos—I sent you a composite yesterday . . ."

The teacher smiles, understanding this excitement that can only come once in a dancer's life—the *first* audition.

"And I went to Hopkins Photoservice, as you suggested. They gave me twenty-five reproductions for the price of two 8 × 10 originals . . ."

"You should have a negative that you can reorder from," the teacher reminds gently.

"The man was so nice . . ."

You've spent a lifetime thinking, thinking, thinking about a professional career—a goal that's blossomed with each year of your life. And now it's taken shape, and all you have to do is reach out and grasp it. You've spent the past two years researching for whom and where you'd like to dance; company after company you've examined, analyzed, questioned, discarded some, pursued others. You've attended summer programs, and you've listened as professional dancers have tried to mold your aspirations into workable form. You have your résumé, your photos, and your high-school-class release tabime under control, you have your determination and your confidence pinging with resolve.

Now you are ready for the auditions. You've written to some companies and maybe they haven't responded. What to do?

Use the telephone. Ask to speak to the company manager or stage manager. Where and when are the auditions, you want to know, what salary range, how many dancers in the company, what are the repertory and the projected performances for the following season. Information is all you seek. Have a pen and a piece of paper handy; write down what they tell you.

The New York scene is easiest as far as gaining information is concerned. There are audition boards at the major studios, including School of American Ballet and the Joffrey School. The boards list all the auditions in the city as well as those outside New York. Every Thursday *Backstage* (a newspaper) comes out, and it too lists available auditions.

If you really can't get to New York, the best thing, aside from personal contact with the company directors and continual checking with your local dance studios, is to keep a close watch on the monthly display advertisements and classified insertions in *Dance Magazine*. Since *Dance* is a monthly magazine, its ads are not as current as those in a newspaper like *Backstage,* but it can be useful anyway.

Audition day finally comes.

- Prepare two or three pairs of pointe shoes in case one pair doesn't work; don't use pointe shoes that haven't been broken in.

- Never wear elastic around your hips, or if you insist on wearing some, make sure it is a dark color (light-colored elastic will distract the auditioner).

- A clean, unfrayed chiffon skirt should only be used for center work, not at the barre. (You want the auditioner to get a proper look at your body, don't you?)

- A dark-colored leotard and pink tights is the *only* proper audition attire. Although traditionally black was the color, a sea of black can make an audition very difficult for the director; a color will make you stand out. Never wear junk!

- It never hurts to wear pretty perfume; it can make you feel good, and it might be the one special thing a director remembers about you!

- Your attitude is crucial; directors don't want troublemakers. Enjoy your audition; think of it as a performance (because it really is).

Suppose you have an audition scheduled and you are injured? *Don't let it prevent you from attending the audition!* Even if you are sporting a huge ace-type bandage, write a short note to the director, and make sure you hand it directly to him or her, telling when you were injured, that it is not a recurring injury, that you are under a physician's care, and that you expect the injury to clear up in so many days or weeks.

Don't let the auditioners forget you. Don't you forget them, either.

An elastic around the hips or waist cuts up a lovely line and can be distracting to the auditioner. Pamela Whitehill.

The major audition season is from late January through May each year. Although some artistic directors audition throughout the country, most prefer to do their auditioning from their home studios or to set up a major area-wide audition in New York City or Los Angeles. The reasons are obvious, of course. The large population centers offer a major talent pool, and for out-of-town dancers there is less hardship in getting to New York or Los Angeles.

But if you come to New York, especially remember this: you still need to make further contact with the companies you are interested in because there is so much dance activity, so many dancers, and so elusive a dance schedule. Things change in New York . . . fast! Once you arrive in the city, check and double-check your audition time, date, and location, even though you may have received a letter or phone call barely one week before.

Then, allow yourself an hour or two and visit the main studios such as Broadway Arts, Steps 74th, or David Howard's school and the larger dance-wear shops such as Taffy's, Freeds, or Capezio. Check their bulletin boards because you could find an audition call you may have missed.

But perhaps you don't wish to come to New York—at least not now. No problem at all. Go to the *Performing Arts Guide* and select the companies and locations that appeal to you elsewhere in the country. Once you've got your photos in hand, they should be sent out—along with your résumé—to every company that makes your list.

Auditions can follow any of several formats, but probably the most dreaded—and the most available—is the "cattle call." Here, every dancer is given a number as soon as she or he arrives at the studio or theatre. At the appropriate moment the artistic director sweeps in and arranges the dancers in one or more lines. "Walk from stage left to stage right," will be the command, and as each dancer passes, the artistic director will signal to an assistant or the ballet master or mistress, who will then dismiss or retain the dancer according to the artistic director's decision.

Arbitrary? Of course it is.

Whimsical? Possibly.

What's happening is that the field is being narrowed purely on look, a lightning-fast appraisal based on the director's certainty of what he or she needs *on the most superficial level*. Don't mistake this for an in-depth rendering of your ultimate ballet skill or true physical grace.

It is simply the director's first cut, a winnowing of the field. Think of it this way: if you don't look right to the director, then whatever ballet skill you possess will never quite fit with what the director is seeking to produce. You will always be figuratively out of step.

So the director starts with a look, and by the time the process is concluded roughly forty percent of those who answered the cattle call have been eliminated. Then begins appraisal of ballet technique.

The remaining dancers are sent to the barre and given pliés on one side, tendus on the other . . . over and over. Gradually the director can see which turnout, which feet merit approval, and after this exercise, another elimination occurs. A further twenty percent will go.

That leaves about forty percent of the original audition, and now things move more rapidly. The director will call for movement to develop extension (ten percent leave), adage in the center, balance, and musicality (another ten percent leave), and finally pirouettes, petit and grand allégro, which reduces the field by still another ten percent.

Now there are only a few dancers left (perhaps you are among them), and you will be asked to don pointe shoes and pair up with one of the males who has also survived elimination.

And what if the male has trouble with your height?

Talk to him about how to adapt. For instance, he can try to hold your forearm instead of your hand for turns and promenades.

But talk to him, communicate with him, do not let things go. You are partners, even for only a brief moment, and it's to your mutual advantage to make it work the best it can.

Often, there's a question about . . . *what to wear!* Should I be different, should I try to stand out, will they notice me if I wear something unusual? The quick answer is to remember that one of the beauties of classical ballet is its uniformity, its cohesion. To stand out for no purpose other than to gain attention is not appropriate.

So, what do you wear? A dark rose leotard would be nice, or a navy or emerald one.

In the end there's much more to how you fare at an audition than what you are wearing. Robert Barnett of the Atlanta Ballet puts it succinctly: "I look for personality and a dancer's body," he says, "I want a positive outlook and a sense of awareness." He says nothing about the type of leotard you might be wearing, or about any other particle of clothing that may be about your body. He is looking at the total you, and he won't be deflected by pizzazz.

There are other types of auditions than the cattle call—elimination by a simple look. One is where the director waits until barre work is in progress and then begins the elimination process. It might happen during barre exercise, then a second elimination after the barre . . . or after adage, pirouettes, grand allégro, pas de deux, and even pointe work. Here the director is interested in your *ballet* skill and technique, though, of course, the way you look will play a part in all that. But at least the way you look won't automatically send you to the sidelines.

From the dancer's standpoint the most satisfying audition is one where the director makes no attempt to eliminate anyone during the entire class. He or she watches carefully, noting strengths and weaknesses, but no one is singled out until class is finished. Then the director—or ballet master or mistress—quietly asks certain dancers to stay for "call-back," while the remainder of the class is eliminated.

"Call-back" means basically what it says—a dancer is invited to return and reaudition, usually an hour and a half or so after the end of the regular audition. It is a second chance at one of the available jobs, and only a few people are chosen for this. When a call-back audition occurs, however, it does not consist of the usual company class (barre and center work). Instead, male and female dancers are paired for pas de deux.

You should be ready if and when you receive a call-back audition. Spend the time between the auditions re-energizing yourself; find a warm place to relax, eat a yogurt, or drink some fruit juice (remember—no caffeine!). Lie on your back with feet up, but be sure to stay warm. Twenty minutes before you have to return, do some barre work and stretch so you are ready to continue the audition.

At the call-back audition things will happen quickly. You will be given a partner—it might be someone you've never met before so introduce yourself quietly and try to find some instant rapport, some quick understanding. Remember, you both have been called back, so you have to work for and with one another. If, for example, you have partnering problems such as jumping out or overarching, discuss this immediately and ask your partner to do the same. You will save yourself mistakes that could cost either or both of you an injury and/or the audition.

Don't be surprised when auditions are advertised and conducted for women only or men only. This allows the director to concentrate more directly on the way his corps de ballet might look. But men and women are put together when call-backs are announced.

Don't be surprised if you are asked whether you are a member of the American Guild of Musical Artists. Usually, union companies (and most major companies have union affiliation) are required to hire union dancers *first* because of their union contracts (see more about this in "Contracts and Unions," in chap. 3), but even if they aren't, union companies are used to looking at union dancers first, and this will be the procedure they follow. But if, after that first audition, the company doesn't see a union dancer they want, they will go to the nonunion dancers.

Arrive at your audition at least forty-five minutes in advance and register as soon as you arrive. The earlier you arrive the lower the number you will receive, and the lower the number, the closer you will be to the front of the studio.

What's the advantage?

Not only will you be more visible, but you will be able to see and hear the combinations more clearly. Directors have little patience with dancers—especially at auditions—who don't follow properly.

Most auditioners issue numbers, written in magic marker on a piece of white paper (which invariably disintegrates as you perspire). It never hurts to carry a few safety pins so you can attach the number, *but don't be cute and put the number on an offensive part of your anatomy.* Pin it to the front of your leotard at the neck V or on your tee shirt in such a way that it is clearly visible.

Girls should,

• have clean *pink* tights (never wear black).

• have a clean and neat leotard in a pretty color (wine, rose, dark emerald, soft rose, medium blue). Recently, female dancers have been arriving in traditional black; this makes it difficult for the auditioner to gauge ballet skill and technique because of the sameness of color.

• *never* wear striped or patterned leotards.

• *never* wear shimmery or shiny miliskin tights—even the slimmest legs looked like stuffed sausages.

• have hair neat and in a bun or braid (no flowers—they are fine for children but not for a professional audition); bangs are all right but make sure they are few and don't flop or bounce when you jump.

• leave jewelry at home—all of it.

• wear attractive street makeup.

Boys should,

• wear clean black or gray tights and a snug-fitting white T shirt or matching tank-top leotard worn under the tights.

• wear a belt to hold the tights neatly.

• wear black or white ballet shoes which are clean and neat.

• *never* wear knee sox because they cut the line of the leg.

• *never* wear duct-taped shoes—the auditioner wants to observe the clean, articulated beauty of the unadorned feet.

• have a good haircut that doesn't bounce much when jumping.

Then, perhaps, several weeks after that first audition phone call, the teacher receives another. Same dancer, same excitement, only this time with an air of quiet confidence.

"I've had three good auditions in a row," the dancer says.

The teacher is pleased.

"And one job offer!"

"Wonderful!"

"I could hardly wait to tell you."

In the Company   3

COMPANY STRUCTURE

The purely administrative end and the artistic direction
should be distinct from one another although
maintaining a thoroughly cooperative spirit.
—*Alexander Kahn, patron, Ballet Russe de Monte Carlo*

*T*here really is logic to the way a ballet company is organized, and
even young dancers should be thankful for this area of sanity in
the creative, artistic world of ballet expression. If ballet companies
followed the dictates of whim and personal obsession, organization would
long since have given way to chaos and unrealizable goals. But take heart!
Good sense and long-range planning have established themselves in the
ballet world, and the way a company is organized promotes the best
interests of all—dancers, choreographers, administrators, even the board of
directors.

Basically, the structure of a ballet company follows two separate, though
parallel, paths: artistic, to which you belong, and administrative. These
paths may seem never to converge but actually they are interdependent—
one really can't survive without the other—and so they must be understood
if a young dancer is to achieve maximum benefit as a company member.

Remember this: A ballet company *is* a team, each person has a role to fill,
and the team succeeds only so far as the team members perform their roles
adequately. Public relations people, technical crew, apprentice dancers—
should any let down, the effects are felt by the entire company.

On pages 24 and 25 is a chart of the typical ballet company, and you will
see that the two separate paths—artistic and administrative—follow their
own organizational form. Note who reports to whom, who does not
report to whom, and who has ultimate responsibility for each task.
Following the chart is a brief description of each company position—from

artistic director to stage hand—and the way the person in that position affects you as a young dancer.

This is the breakdown of a *typical* ballet company. There may be variations depending on the company you are most familiar with, but no company strays far from this organizational structure.

The Artistic Staff

Artistic director (AD). Artistic director is the top artistic position, held by a person with vision, the one who sees the company as a whole from rehearsal to performance. She or he hires the ballet master, makes final decisions on the dancers, determines how the company will "look." Will the dancers be tall and skinny, willowy or powerful? The AD chooses the repertoire and decides whether the company will be classical, neoclassical, or contemporary. In many companies the AD is the main choreographer, and if the company is dancing an old classic, she (or he) chooses the person to set that ballet.

Most important to the dancer, an artistic director should be and usually is a mentor, a teacher, and a friend. A good AD can make or break a dance career.

In most small- to medium-size companies, the artistic director sometimes teaches company class. For example, in the Atlanta Ballet, Artistic Director Robert Barnett teaches company-member classes daily on alternate weeks and apprentice classes the other weeks. This way he has constant surveillance of each dancer's progress.

In Ballet de Montréal, AD Eddy Toussaint says of his dancers that they are his "kids" and they dominate his life. "They are the heart of the company." He determines not only their on-stage life but believes that dance is a royal art—he demands a strict dress code whenever his dancers are coming to or going from the theatre or studio.

Most ADs are not this demanding, but you should understand that they tend to become the parent figure in a company and remain a dominant influence on the young dancer.

Ballet master or mistress. This individual is the dancer's main direct contact with his or her art. In smaller companies the ballet master/mistress gives company class; in companies with a substantial apprentice program, he or she may alternate the teaching schedule with the AD.

The ballet master is responsible for rehearsing and cleaning up all performance works under the direction of the artistic director. He also

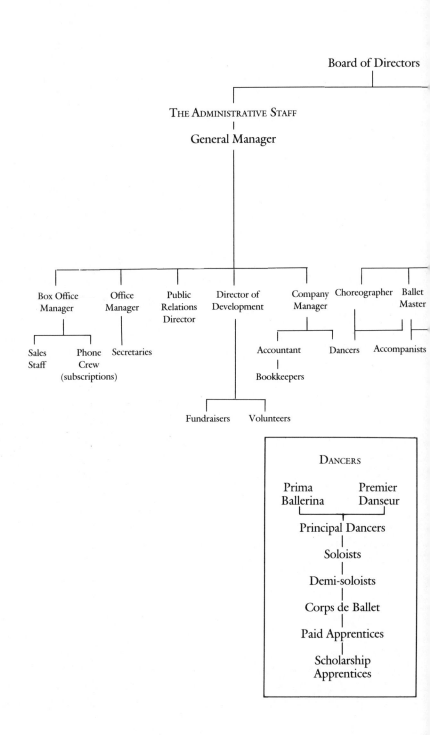

Board of Directors

THE ADMINISTRATIVE STAFF

General Manager

Box Office Manager

Office Manager

Public Relations Director

Director of Development

Company Manager

Choreographer

Ballet Master

Sales Staff

Phone Crew (subscriptions)

Secretaries

Accountant

Dancers

Accompanists

Bookkeepers

Fundraisers

Volunteers

DANCERS

Prima Ballerina

Premier Danseur

Principal Dancers

Soloists

Demi-soloists

Corps de Ballet

Paid Apprentices

Scholarship Apprentices

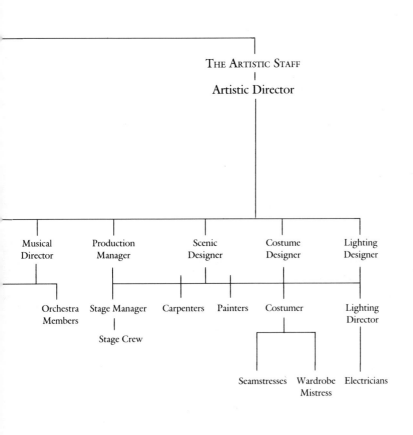

THE ARTISTIC STAFF

Artistic Director

Musical Director

Production Manager

Scenic Designer

Costume Designer

Lighting Designer

Orchestra Members

Stage Manager

Carpenters

Painters

Costumer

Lighting Director

Stage Crew

Seamstresses

Wardrobe Mistress

Electricians

works in conjunction with the stage manager, setting up daily rehearsal schedules.

When a new choreographer or teacher comes to set a ballet, the ballet master works with him or her closely. It is his responsibility to bring that person's work to performance level in exactly the way it was originally taught.

The ballet master must also be aware of the dancer's physical and emotional well-being and ensure that the dancer—if injured or sick—is not pushed (or pushing) too hard, too soon.

Once in the theatre the ballet master gives company class, sits with the AD and choreographer during rehearsal, takes notes and corrections, delivers them to the dancers, and implements them.

Choreographer. The choreographer is responsible for creating and setting works the dancers perform. Some companies have a resident choreographer. In others the AD is the primary choreographer, but most companies also bring in choreographers to set new or special works.

The choreographer auditions the dancers (by either watching class or giving pieces of his work to them to see how they handle it) and, with the AD and ballet master, decides on casting. Visiting choreographers usually spend a week or two setting their work, returning to the company just prior to the premier performance to help with last minute "cleaning."

Musical director. The musical director is in charge of the orchestra and accompanists. Often this person is also the conductor of the orchestra, and his major responsibility is to see that the AD and ballet master have rehearsal recordings at the correct and same tempo as the orchestra will play in performance. Musical directors usually sit in on studio rehearsals to ensure correct tempos. They learn the idiosyncrasies and strengths of the dancers so they can hold the orchestra when a dancer hits a particularly secure balance, or speed the music up to show off a virtuosic dance or even challenge a dancer with a spontaneous variation.

At an orchestra rehearsal of Atlanta Ballet's *Nutcracker* on tour, the musical director decided to have a little fun with James Lee, one of the Candy Canes, and he prepared a little surprise. On closing night, when the traditional choreography is often played with, the musical director conducted the orchestra at double time as James Lee took the stage. Lee took the challenge, dancing as fast as he could, and finished the variation with a triple jump through the hoop!

The musical director is also responsible for hiring and maintaining a pool of accompanists who play for class daily and for ensuring that the accompanists understand the musical demands of the artistic director and/or ballet master.

Production manager (PM). The production manager oversees all aspects of the production and is responsible for coordinating the dancing with scenery, lighting, and costume. The production manager hires all stage crew, dressers, and union personnel, but he is less responsible for the actual running of the show, the stage part of it, than he is for pulling together all of the nuts and bolts of running the production.

At dress rehearsal the PM sits with the AD, ballet master, and designers and takes notes on the timing of the program and the running of set changes, cues, and all aspects of the performance. Often the PM will "call" the show on opening night, although this job usually belongs to the stage manager.

A dancer's first contact with the PM is when his or her theatre cases are given out. If at any time the dancer needs to get something from one of the trucks, he or she would go to the PM. Major technical problems on the set are overseen by the PM and worked out with the scenic, lighting, and costume designers.

Lighting, scenic, and costume designers. Each ballet needs specific lighting, sets, and costumes. In some cases the artistic director employs free-lance designers for a new ballet; they create their designs and send them to the production manager, who oversees their creation and use. But sometimes the designer comes to oversee the completion and use prior to the first performance.

Often a choreographer selects or recommends designers. If the ballet has been danced by another company, the original designs may be used.

In companies that have resident costumers and lighting directors, these personnel design to the choreographer's specifications but always under the overall supervision of the production manager and artistic director.

Stage manager. The stage manager is the liaison between the production staff and artistic staff. He or she is responsible for "calling" the show—standing in the "prompt" corner and giving cues to lighting and other crew. The stage manager tells the conductor when to go to the podium or runs the sound system when there is no orchestra. The stage manager is responsible for informing dancers how long before the curtain rises; he is also responsible for finding out why a dancer or performer missed a cue.

The stage manager's job also includes checking the studios (tape on floors isn't ripped, barres are secure, pianos are in tune, sound and video equipment is available and working).

He is responsible for the dancers' rehearsal and costume fitting schedules, which he coordinates with the AD, ballet master, and costumer. In a well-run company the rehearsal schedules are posted one day in advance; they must be posted twenty-four hours in advance in a union company. He also schedules photo shoots.

The stage manager ensures that the person leading rehearsal has the right music (on tape) and videos of the ballet when needed. He is also responsible for making tapes if the dancer needs them.

In small companies the stage manager often handles some of the company manager's duties. In other situations the company manager hires a stage manager just for the performance and assumes the "in-studio" duties of a stage manager on a day-to-day basis.

Lighting director/technician. Without the lighting director the audience would never see the dancers. His responsibility is to translate the lighting design, maintain the company's lights (or rent them), make sure the lights are packed carefully into road boxes for touring and that they are "hung" and circuited correctly.

The lighting technician usually runs the lights from the lighting booth. He sets the cues before the company arrives at the theatre. With the help of the crew he makes sure all the lights are focused properly. Occasionally, in smaller companies, a dancer might be asked to stand on stage while the crew focuses one or two lights. He or she will be asked to stand in a certain spot on stage, all the lights will be turned off, then one light will be turned on. A crew member will manually adjust the light in the cove until the light on the dancer is clear and well defined. This process is repeated with every light on and off stage and can take many hours (sometimes all day).

Costumer. The costumer can be one of the dancer's best friends. She is responsible for every article of clothing a dancer wears on stage as well as for ordering and maintaining a ready supply of shoes and tights for the dancers.

In many companies, the costumer is also the primary costume designer and works closely with the AD and choreographers. She often attends rehearsal so she can see the quality and intent of the choreography and how the dancers move and interact. She is responsible for choosing designs and fabrics, and buys all fabrics, trims, notions, and equipment to construct costumes and headdresses.

The costumer has complete responsibility in the costume shop. She hires the wardrobe mistress, cutters, and seamstresses and oversees construction of all costumes; it is to her the dancer complains if a seamstress leaves a pin in a costume—not an uncommon occurrence!

In one major ballet company, seventeen beautiful tutus had been built for *Paquita*. Each one was checked and rechecked for pins. When the costumes were taken to the cleaners six weeks later, two pins were found deep in the layers of net, though the dancer wearing the costume never complained.

The costumer is responsible for keeping the sewing inventory intact, for keeping the machinery in working order, and for making sure the costume road boxes are clean and maintained.

The costumer must estimate the shoes and tights needed by each dancer and order the required amount to be delivered at intervals during the season. She must also be aware of each dancer's use pattern so that the allowance is not abused (see page 61).

The costumer oversees the packing of the costumes, and it is her responsibility if part of a costume is left or lost in the theatre. If the company is touring a ballet that uses "supers" or children in each city, the costumer goes on ahead of the company to fit the costumes, so that any changes can be made.

Orchestra and accompanists. All professional companies use accompanists for daily class. In some instances the main accompanist also plays in the orchestra and uses a company piano score to play in rehearsals. It is unusual for a company to have its own full-time orchestra. While the same musicians may play for all ballet performances, they will perform with other groups as well (opera, symphony, musicals, etc.).

Wardrobe mistress. The wardrobe mistress is a full-time employee and very important to the dancer. She issues the dancer's shoes, tights, and costumes and is responsible for packing the costumes on tour and making sure the dressers know which piece goes with which costume and that each costume is properly ironed and repaired. The wardrobe mistress is responsible for making sure that the assigned dresser is in the wings for all fast changes, and in many instances she will be there as a backup.

In the studio the wardrobe mistress works closely with the costumer. She cuts, sews, and fits and often oversees the construction of costumes for a new ballet. In companies where there is no costumer, the wardrobe mistress fulfills all these duties too. The wardrobe mistress is in charge of union dressers and seamstresses.

Dressers. The dressers arrive at the theatre a day before the dancers and work with the wardrobe mistress unpacking, ironing, and repairing each costume piece. They deliver the costumes to the dressing room. During rehearsal and performance they are with the dancers, helping them get into and out of their costumes. Dressers must know all fast changes and when and where they occur, and then be there with all costume pieces and shoes. Dressers always carry two needles threaded with black and white thread, scissors, pins, tape, extra ribbon, elastic, and any other repair supply.

Because dance is so physical, costumes rip and tear often. Even though the wardrobe mistress and dressers check them carefully before each performance, occasionally a costume rips or tears on stage. Dressers must be ready to mend and fix in a flash.

Stage hands. The movie image of old men playing poker in the wings while the show goes on is sheer fantasy. Stage hands are hardworking people who must be strong and alert. It is their responsibility to move scenery and work the rigging which controls the cyc, scrims, drops, and flown scenery pieces. They load and unload all the trucks.

The Dancers' Ladder

Prima ballerina or premier danseur. These titles are given only to dancers of extraordinary talent and great artistry. Often the prima and premier danseur will dance as guest artists.

Some companies are very small . . . and others are large. Left: Vermont Ballet Theatre. © Dana Jenkins; right: Boston Ballet, Bruce Marks, artistic director. © Jack Mitchell.

Principal dancers. Principal dancers dance the main roles, such as Giselle, Swan Queen, Aurora, Titania, and so forth, and the leads in neoclassical and contemporary works.

Soloists. Soloists dance the next most important roles, such as Myrta, Lilac Fairy, and Princesses (act 1, *Swan Lake*). They often take over from principals.

Demi-soloists. Demi-soloists dance solo roles within the corps, such as Little and Big Swans in *Swan Lake* (act 2), friends in *Coppélia,* Red Riding Hood, and character roles. These parts are usually danced with two to four other dancers.

Corps de ballet. Members dance the main corps (group) parts, such as swans, wilis, villagers, snowflakes, and flowers. They understudy demi-soloist and soloist roles and occasionally dance them on tour.

Apprentice dancers. Apprentices are the youngest, newest dancers, usually in their first professional job. They dance with the corps de ballet, often in the least conspicuous place. Only on the rarest occasions do they receive soloist or demi-soloist roles.

The Administrative Staff

General manager. The general manager is the liaison between artistic, production, and administrative staffs and the board of directors. He is responsible for finding and budgeting the finances with which to run the company. He works directly with the board of directors, often suggesting new members whom he feels will be able to bring additional fund-raising capability. He works with booking agents and sponsors to solidify tours. He works with the AD on budgets which he then takes to the board of directors, who then raise the necessary funds. He is the company image in the business/financial community.

Company manager. The company manager deals with the dancers' contracts, health insurance, worker's compensation, per diem, and all other financial matters that affect the dancers.

"A company manager's work happens during curtain/performance time. While the stage manager is in the prompt corner, the company manager should be in the box office, counting tickets, writing checks, doing the payroll, and doing the paperwork dealing with tonight's performance. He is responsible for the bus and the dancers and musicians on the bus," says Taffy Waters, a production manager who has worked with British, Canadian, and U.S. companies.

Public relations director. The public relations director is responsible for the media image and for making the public aware of performances. He supervises advertising and promotional activities and arranges for individual publicity appearances. He is responsible for communicating the company's activities to the general public and arranges newspaper, television, and radio interviews and photo calls.

Development/fund-raising. This department works with the general manager and board of directors to help raise funds. It also directs volunteers for fund-raising, public imaging, and the like. In smaller companies this responsibility falls equally on the general manager, company manager, and public relations department.

Box office manager. Most well-organized companies have a box office at the studio, where the general public can purchase tickets or subscriptions prior to performances. The box office manager is responsible for ordering tickets (that match the seating numbers in any given theatre), selling seats and subscriptions, and assigning volunteers to such theatre duties as ushering, taking tickets, selling refreshments, and so forth.

Volunteers. Volunteers are members of the community who have a particular love of dance and are willing to help the company without pay. They can be seen working as ushers, selling refreshments, telephoning the general public to sell subscriptions, and helping at fund-raising parties, in public relations, or anywhere else their interest lies. Every good company has a steady stream of volunteers.

Like any other well-run organization, there are receptionists, secretaries, accountants, and bookkeepers who perform the same tasks as they would in the corporate world.

CONTRACTS AND UNIONS

> *There are very fine companies who are union and vice-versa.*
> —*Richard Englund, artistic director, Joffrey II*

A contract is a contract is a contract . . . Right?
Wrong!

Contracts differ from ballet company to ballet company, sometimes even from dancer to dancer. Does a member of the corps de ballet expect to receive the same treatment as a soloist? Will the Joffrey contract provide the same perquisites as the contract of the Omaha Ballet Company?

No, of course not. Each is different; each has certain special areas of coverage, certain peculiar concerns, certain areas of expertise that must be acknowledged. A written contract is by far the clearest and fairest way of doing that.

Young professionals live and die by what their contracts say, and it simply makes good sense to read *and* understand the words and the paragraphs. You want to know if you're being rehearsed too much . . . read your contract; you want to know whether you can take a train instead of a plane when going on tour . . . read your contract; you want to know the maximum number of performances you can be asked to do in a week . . . read your contract.

Train yourself to think contract! If you have signed it, then you better understand you are bound by what the contract says. A dispute with the ballet master arises . . . reach for the contract.

Know what you have signed. There isn't a better test of your seriousness as a dancer than your awareness of what you can and cannot do under your company contract. This is where maturity takes over because once you reach the age of eighteen, you are no longer an "infant" in the eyes of the law (don't take this too literally—"infant" is a legal term of art that refers to anyone under eighteen). This means you are presumed to understand what you have signed because you are now an adult and subject to the standards adults must answer to.

It means, for example, that you can't complain you didn't understand the contract should something happen that you didn't plan for (such as running out of sick leave). You can't complain that no one offered to explain certain provisions to you. Unless there has been outright fraud (and this is pretty rare in a reputable company), it's up to you to seek out the help you need. You are an adult, remember (at least in the eyes of the law), and that means having a sense of self-responsibility. If you don't understand . . . ask! If you aren't sure . . . ask! If you think there's a mistake . . . ask!

A contract is nothing more than an agreement between two consenting minds, but once signed, it controls your relationship with the company you dance with.

The following, or a minor variation of it, is the way most dancer-company contracts begin, and it is pretty straightforward.

This agreement made this	day of

, 19   , by and between

(hereinafter, DANCER) and

(hereinafter, COMPANY)

W I T N E S S E T H

1. COMPANY agrees to . . . . .

2. DANCER agrees to . . . . .

A contract describes rights and duties, both yours and the company's, so each paragraph spells out one or the other. In the appendix to this book you will find an apprenticeship contract. Paragraphs two, three, and four of that contract begin:

• "Apprentice agrees . . . "

• "The Ballet agrees . . . "

• "The Apprentice understands . . . "

These paragraphs describe rights and duties, and every contract you sign, whether as apprentice or full company member, will have them. Read further in the contract and note the categories of additional rights and duties (remember—both you *and* the company have rights and duties in a contract; it is not a one-way street):

• performances, classes, and rehearsals

• illness

• dismissal

• makeup

• travel

And note too the section titled "Other Duties" listing your additional duties as an apprentice member of the company and the company's right to ask you to perform them.

A contract is a combination of rights and duties; understand that and you understand why the contract is much more important than simply an agreement about how much you are to be paid. The contract is your passport to equitable treatment as a dancer and to achieving your career expectations. It is not, however, a license to demand more than you have agreed to, nor is it written in stone. You perform well, you abide by the contract provisions, and the contract will protect you. You ignore those provisions, you violate them, and the contract will protect the company *at your expense.*

No one really wants that to happen.

By far the most prevalent type of contract arrangement—at least with the major U.S. companies—is the union company. That is, the dancers are represented by the union in their dealings with company management; the union (of which you would be a member) negotiates for the dancers on most work-related matters and settles things such as rehearsal hours, travel limitations, and seniority.

Dancers belong to AGMA, the American Guild of Musical Artists; it is a national union in the sense that it covers dancers from San Francisco to Boston, no matter the company, no matter the city. When you join a union company, it means that AGMA has local union representation where you work, and the company recognizes that AGMA represents you, the dancer.

AGMA negotiates a standard contract with dance companies through-out the United States. (Simultaneously, of course, the dance companies are part of an organization too, so it is their organization that negotiates with AGMA.) This contract then becomes the standard reference for most work-related matters in your company, and your employment contract will include those provisions.

Is there an alternative to the union company?

Absolutely. There are a number of nonunion companies, many of them small, where the dancers are not affiliated with anyone. Obviously, if you are in one of these companies, you must expect to wage more of your own employment battles because there may not be anyone with big clout ready to go to the mat on your account. The nonunion company, however, does have the advantage of bringing you into closer contact with company management, and you may find this to your liking.

But . . . a big but. The question of union or nonunion company status should not be the single deciding factor on whether you join a certain company. It's more important to spark off your career, and if that can be done with one particular company, then you shouldn't worry unduly about union or nonunion status. Note what well-regarded ballet teacher David Howard says about it: "I think that in terms of the contract, the most important thing is to look at the company rather than to look and see whether they are union or nonunion. I think it's important for the dancer to start, to get going, and not to be too concerned about anything else. I would think of it in terms of . . . look at the company, look at what they're doing." After this, he advises, will come the time to weigh the union affiliation. "What benefits are there in terms of being unionized?" he suggests you ask yourself. Does the union add benefits or take them away?

And, almost as an afterthought, he mentions, "Some of the companies run themselves very well along union lines, *and they may not be unionized.*"

In other words, the dancers act as if they were in a union, they speak as if they were in a union, they follow the work rules set up by a union . . . but they don't belong to a union!

Impossible? Not at all. If, for example, company management is willing to recognize the terms and conditions that AGMA has negotiated even if there is no AGMA affiliation in your company, then you have this precise situation. You refer to the AGMA standard contract for your rights and duties, and you should be guided accordingly.

Only remember this! You have to fight your own battles more readily in a nonunion company. It becomes you against management, more personalized, more direct.

Robert Barnett, artistic director of the Atlanta Ballet, puts the matter quite succinctly. He is not a strong supporter of unions; in fact, he says, "if they were good, there would be more companies with unions than there are." Yet he also recognizes the value of a union-type structure even in his nonunion company. "We obey the union rules," he says, "as far as working schedules and salaries are concerned." A nonunion company that acts like a union company but really isn't.

Generally, though, salaries are less in nonunion companies, and this can be a determining factor for some young dancers. But as Arthur Leeth of the Boston Ballet points out, just because you may be in a union company doesn't mean you will be getting top dollar. "It depends on the size of the company," he says. "Our company, for example, offers less salary than a company in New York but far more than a union company in Michigan or Salt Lake City." There are benefits, he believes, to working with a nonunion company. "You are not so structurally oriented to certain rehearsal hours [in a nonunion company], but with a union there are specific hours when you can rehearse, when you can't rehearse, when you must be on, when you have to be off." He acknowledges that sometimes it's worthwhile for a company to carefully structure hours in this way because otherwise the organization can take advantage of the dancer, since there would be no one to object on the dancer's behalf. At the same time, though, he sees that some union rules actually hold the young dancer back. "For example," he says, "the union has a rule that if you have three hours of rehearsal, you must have one hour off. But where you only have one more hour left in the day, you can waive that hour and get off." What he means is that this last hour might be used for work, especially on a current piece, but the dancers could simply insist on their break time, leave the studio, and return in the morning. The rehearsal would have to pick up the pieces from what was left the day before, instead of concentrating on something else.

Unions and union contracts must be understood by every young professional who is serious about a career in dance. It may not be so important *at this moment* for you (because you're in a nonunion company), but before your dance days are finished, you will come up against union rules and procedures, and you will probably sign a union contract.

Tis better to be forearmed . . .

What you will find is that a number of experienced dance professionals have distinct and often negative views on the value of AGMA and union affiliation. But understand their motivations: they are usually part of management, and so it is their job to blunt union requests for changes and improvements in dancers' work rules, especially when these items will cost the company money. Unions are a thorn in management's side; they work for the dancer, and often what is in the dancer's interest may not be in the company's interest.

Take Rochelle Zide Booth, for instance. She has seen things from both sides of the table—as a dancer and as a company executive—and her views about a national union such as AGMA are clear. "I don't think the union can address what an individual company or individual dancer needs," she says, implying that a national union loses touch with the grass roots concerns of the individual dancer. "You are contracted to work x amount of hours for x amount of money, and that's the maximum amount of hours you can work. I mean . . . choreographers can be in the middle of the greatest piece of choreography they have ever done, and your union tells you that you have to walk out the door at that moment because it's time for you to stop working." For her, this represents a terrible blow to creativity, and she believes that it makes dancers less dedicated.

But she also sees the current situation as a normal progression from an earlier, more difficult period. "There was a time," she says, "when unions were necessary, when dancers were completely at the mercy of the artistic director. But that is not the case anymore."

Her views are echoed by Richard Englund, artistic director of Joffrey II, who sees union affiliation as having less to do with the company's ultimate performance product than with the administrative load that can end up costing more money. "Many times a union contract can be burdened with issues that are outdated or no longer necessary," he says, "and they can make a situation so rigid that the company and the dancer can suffer and not have as good an artistic relationship." Certain rehearsal demands are one example. Union contracts are very specific about hours, and they are rigidly enforced. In the current AGMA–National Dance Agreement note these two simple provisions:

- The ARTIST shall be given one 5-minute break during each hour of rehearsal. . . .

- ARTISTS must have one and one-half (1-1/2) hours off between rehearsals called at two (2) different studio or theatre locations if such locations are more than one-half (1/2) mile apart.

Suppose a choreographer is setting a major piece and a crucial movement is building. Might a rehearsal break not interrupt the creative energy and stall the ultimate product? Can choreographers turn creativity on and off like a water faucet?

Bending creativity to these union rules is what Richard Englund means when he talks of the rigidity of the union contract. It can also affect the dancer, however, especially one who may be locked into a corps or ensemble contract. The choreographer chooses the dancer to work on and then the union rules are invoked. "Sometimes an artist, or an emerging artist, is prevented from having the kind of experience that would be most productive even if they have been in the company for a long time," he says, adding that he would hope some flexibility might be adopted in the way the dancer and the choreographer and the union would approach things. "Now I'm not saying that someone has to be taken off and worked with for ten hours in a row. I'm just saying maybe it isn't time to have that break."

But the union would respond that such protections are for *all* dancers, that choreographers need to schedule their work better, that exceptions, such as they are, could be considered.

In a dispute like this where do you turn? The answer is simple: you have your own union representatives, two and sometimes three per company, chosen by you and the other dancers. These representatives are company members too, dancers just as you, and they are the ones to see if you have an initial complaint. Some companies insist that an apprentice be one of the union representatives, especially where there are a large number of apprentices in the company. At the least, though, you will have other dancers representing your interests when the union meets with the company.

In the meantime, the union contract stands as the only monolith that will protect dancers from company abuse, overuse, and exploitation. There may be flaws in the overall approach, but it is doubtful that dancers could enjoy job protection and work rule coverages to the extent they have now without the union slogging away in the trenches year after year.

APPRENTICESHIP AGONISTES

> *It's a time to hear music, see the lights and grow, a time*
> *to make mistakes you will never make again.*
> —*Teresina Goheen, dancer, Tulsa Ballet*

Ah ha, the mind whirls . . . my first job, I'm a professional, the years of work, that guidance counselor who never believed I'd do it, Mom and Dad will be so proud. MY FIRST JOB! I won't have to worry about college, I'll be making money, I'll have a career, I'll dance with famous people. MY FIRST JOB! I wonder how the famous primas felt at a time like this . . .

I'm so scared. Apprentice . . . company . . . professional . . . Do they *really* think I'm good enough?

Such is the suffering flip-flop a young ballet company apprentice goes through. There is unbounded thrill—I made it! Hard work and years of trying and I made it!

There is that nagging terror—I'm not strong enough, look at the extension on those company dancers! They are so beautiful!

The truth is, if you've been offered an apprenticeship contract by a recognized company, it's not because they have warm milk flowing through their veins, nor is it because they flipped a coin and you came up heads.

They want you because you're good and because you will fit ballet-wise with the other dancers. Simple as that . . . though seventeen- and eighteen-year-olds sometimes have trouble believing it.

An apprenticeship contract is a professional contract in every sense of the word. You will be dancing and getting paid for it, but at the same time you will also be learning to improve your skills. In short, an apprenticeship contract is actually two separate arrangements: on the surface it is exactly what it purports to be—a contract between you and the company which will pay you money to dance and perform. But there is also a second understanding: while you agree to fill out the roles the company assigns to you, the company also promises to *teach* you the finer, more subtle points of classical ballet, to provide you with a training opportunity so your ballet talent can grow and develop.

As an apprentice you will be *learning*, and you will be doing it under the watchful eyes of experienced, highly trained professionals.

That is what apprenticeship means, and that is what apprenticeship can provide.

But the experience, for all its obvious benefits, is never easy. You will be at the bottom of the skill ladder in the company; you may be paid much less than anyone else in the company except for other apprentices; you will be younger than anyone else; you will be given roles that no one else may want. But you will be dancing every day in a professional company, learning new roles, performing. A dream come true.

Yes, you are a professional, and perhaps you may console yourself by believing that most everyone started this way. The real test is how long you plan to remain on that bottom ladder rung, how quickly you can establish yourself as a dancer with a solid future. For the truth is this: in companies which have apprenticeship programs, a savvy artistic director is always on the lookout for talent, and sometimes such talent is growing in the backyard.

Here's Robert Barnett of the Atlanta Ballet: "Our apprenticeship program gives me the chance to observe and see how a dancer works in a way I might not see in an audition. In our program they get a lot of performing, and it gives them a chance to see if they are happy with our company."

And, by implication, it gives Barnett and the Atlanta Ballet the chance to see if they wish the apprentice to remain in the company. A two-way street, of course, a two-level arrangement.

In Atlanta, as in some other medium-sized companies, young dancers may be offered a scholarship apprenticeship in lieu of a full apprenticeship. This means they do not receive a regular salary, though they will receive a per diem allowance and hotel expenses when they dance and tour with the company. In all other respects, however, they operate as full company apprentices. They take company class every day (for free!), and they audition alongside company members for choreographers who are casting a new ballet.

Occasionally, in fact, an apprentice or scholarship apprentice is cast over a company member. Annette Maynard, formerly a principal dancer with the Ballet Iowa, remembers such a time. A guest choreographer had been hired, and the artistic director decided to let the choreographer work unimpeded. "We came to a point where we had four girls all the same height . . . and then there was me—only four-feet eleven—and another girl five-foot seven. Either of us was going to wreck the corps line, so one of us was going to have to be the soloist in the new piece. They gave a petit allégro, which is my forte, and I was able to show my work well. I got the soloist role even though I was only eighteen and an apprentice."

Ahhh, you say to yourself, but the chance *is* there, isn't it?

Opportunity, that old scroundrel, should never be denied. Yet realism is the healthier alternative, and for apprenticeships it is better to deal with more pragmatic concerns . . . such as dance clothes and ballet shoes. These, along with living expenses and recreational pursuits, are your responsibility. That is, when you work for a company as an apprentice—whether you are a scholarship apprentice or paid apprentice—you must pay for these things yourself. It is only at performance time that the company might—note *might*—provide you with shoes and tights. Otherwise the expenses are yours.

Two years is about the limit for scholarship apprentice work. If you stay longer than that, you are just hurting yourself and your career. Two years and no paid apprenticeship offer—poof! you're gone. Look elsewhere; you are obviously in the wrong company, *not* the wrong business! Get that straight! Your style, your body type, your height just don't work in this company. That doesn't mean such things won't work with another company. Remember these words from Arthur Leeth, a ballet master with the Boston Ballet, "None of us [is] suited to dance everywhere in the world, but there will always be a place for you to dance somewhere."

And realize this: in those months you've been a scholarship apprentice, you've learned what it takes to be a professional. Now you can use that knowledge.

Almost all of the major companies have apprentice programs that pay a small, regular salary to those selected. But these are hardly get-rich-quick wages. If you are fortunate enough to be one of these apprentices (and the major companies carry from six to twelve apprentices at any given time), you can expect to be paid under ten thousand dollars per year *gross*! Sometimes it can be below five thousand dollars a year!

Can you live on a salary of one hundred dollars to two hundred dollars per week in a major city without some other kind of help? Can you find lodging and food and transportation and minor recreation on this limited sum?

To say nothing of supplying your own ballet equipment—tights, shoes, skirts, leotards . . .

These are the realities of apprenticeship programs, and most young dancers seek help from their families or friends to bridge this economic chasm. Some major companies include health insurance for their paid apprentices (think of the cost should you be a member of a company which does *not* provide health insurance!), and most supply performance tights and shoes, though not everyday tights and shoes.

Once in a while you can get lucky with lodging. A free boarding facility might be found, and this can go a long way toward liberating your tied-up funds. But don't count on this with most companies. It's really an exception.

One thing you can count on, though . . . at an audition, you will usually have the same opportunities as full company members, and this should not be taken lightly. There are times when an artistic director or choreographer sees just the right body line or movement, and it doesn't matter if the dancer is a full company member or apprentice. What is being sought is an effect, not a title.

Ask a full company member what they remember from their time as an apprentice and chances are one word will sneak out again and again . . . *worry!* The apprentice worries and worries over everything!

"Will they renew my apprenticeship contract?"

"Will they offer me a company contract?"

"Will I be cast as a lead in *Nutcracker*?"

"Is my sore knee really serious?"

"Why is the ballet master so mean to me?"

And so on . . . The point is that as an apprentice your position is the most vulnerable in the company: you have no dance reputation to live up to or to fall back upon; you have no history of fine performing to give you stature or to exact respect. In short, you are now at the beginning of the process of earning your ballet reputation, and as with any other profession, the first steps are often the most difficult to take.

But persevere you must, even if it means worry, worry, worry.

"Why don't they send my apprenticeship contract renewal?" Most companies renew their contracts in May, even though auditions generally take place in February–March. So there is often a six- to eight-week black hole of no-decision before the contract is offered. "Maybe they've changed their minds," you could think . . . "I knew I should have continued to audition" . . . "Now I'll never get a job; it's too late!"

What to do? Call the company manager and ask when the contracts will be sent; if you need more reassurance, ask that he send you a letter of intention to contract, but above all—ask!

"Where shall I stand at the barre?" In companies where apprentices and company members take daily class together (in the largest companies such as the Atlanta Ballet, apprentices have their own class, but there are times when they do take class with other company members, especially in the theatre and on tour), there is the traditional "pecking order," and it comes out most vividly when you face the choice of where to stand at the barre. What it really means is "where do I fit in?" and every young dancer must resolve it somehow. Where dancers stand at the barre is not only a territorial right but the product of seniority and long tradition. Places at the barre are chosen in order of the dancer's importance in the company—primas, soloists, corps members, and finally apprentices. You, the apprentice, get last choice; there's no appeal, no negotiation. You wait until you see where the other dancers stand—or if you are new, you ask another dancer about who stands where—or you wait to be placed by the ballet master.

What you do is observe the manners, courtesy, and traditions of classical ballet . . . as you have been taught to do.

"I don't see why I should learn parts I have no chance of ever dancing!" Ah ha, the apprentice pitfall. Seems to make sense, doesn't it? Why learn something you'll never need? The problem is you never know when never can change. Never is just a word, but circumstances fit an infinite variety of events, and what could be "never" today might be "likely" tomorrow. When you first join the company, the ballet master or artistic director will tell you which parts to learn in which ballets, and from this you may get the impression that you have been "routed" into a certain dance format.

True enough, perhaps, as far as that company is concerned. As a smart apprentice you will spend your spare time watching on video the ballets you've been preparing for or learning the nuances of the parts from another dancer. In short, you will be doing your homework.

Why then would you want to learn any other parts—especially parts you don't think you'll ever dance? The point is . . . you never know! Never. Obviously, this doesn't mean you should try to learn every part available. Show some intelligence. For example, if you're short and cute and comfortable with ingenue parts, you'd be wasting your time learning Profane Love in *Prodigal Son;* if you're a lyrical dancer, there's not much point in learning a staccato ballet. But as a learning process, go beyond the parts officially assigned to you, learn those that you might fit, even if the ballet master hasn't assigned them to you. Try to perfect roles that seem logical for you, even if they haven't yet occurred to the creative dance minds that run the company. Apprenticeship is a learning process, and sometimes the best learning you do can be on your own.

"I never get to dance enough!" One of your most difficult times comes when the company is preparing for a repertory program. Usually these programs include pas de deux and smaller ensemble works, and apprentices are rarely used except as understudies. This means that after morning class you have much of the rest of the day off since the full company members are rehearsing.

It *doesn't* mean, however, that your ballet skills aren't appreciated by the company or that your ballet education should stop. Assuming you don't have a part-time nonballet job or other special interests, you can use this time effectively and perhaps make an additional impression on company management. What about part-time work with company public relations? Or with company costumers or production crews? How about learning other aspects of the ballet art such as video production? Perhaps you might want to get into student teaching or notation . . . maybe even fill in at the box office or as an usher.

All of these opportunities exist to some degree within a company, and while they may not allow you to dance, they do give you a chance to see how your art is transcribed from the narrow dancer's world to the broader public perspective. The dancer who understands that dancing is but one cog in the wheel of a ballet performance is the dancer who has prepared herself or himself for a long ballet career.

Remember: apprenticeship is a time to learn. Those who have come before you understand this; those who stand beside you will help share the experience.

YOU AND THE ARTISTIC DIRECTOR

> *"Now you are a professional, the artistry and the technique must come together always, every day."*
> —Kennet Oberly, artistic director, Ballet Iowa

An artistic director contemplates his company: *These people aren't pulling together, they've tuned out, I need a spark . . .*

"You and you!" he points at two of the newest dancers. "You're ready to understudy the leads in *Sleeping Beauty;* check the schedule tomorrow." He stares fixedly at a demi-soloist. "No more of that cue-missing like last night. It cost at least one curtain call. You're being paid as a professional, act like one." He knows he has the company's attention now, and he surveys them with a hint of disdain. "I want . . . excitement!" He jabs his thumb at one of the male dancers. "Got it?" He doesn't wait for a reply but moves quickly to the other side of the studio by the door. "EXCITEMENT! GIVE . . . ME . . . EXCITEMENT!"

He exits.

One of the dancers, not singled out, tries to control her outrage. *Bully!* she thinks. *He has no right to talk like that! We're not animals, not trash on the street. If he wants professional attitude, professional work, he better treat us like professionals . . .* WHO DOES HE THINK HE IS?

She stomps her foot on the studio floor, loud enough so heads turn. She grins to cover her embarrassment.

A dichotomy is what we have: two points of view covering the same occurrence, contradictory in approach, contradictory in effect. What the artistic director sees, what he says, what the dancer hears him say, what she sees him do are the same. But their reactions are different.

This is the essence of the artistic director–dancer relationship: both want the company to perform well, both want to succeed, both want audience after audience to cheer them endlessly. Yet each brings to the relationship something different. Something needed, to be sure, but different. For example, the artistic director might bring his desire for a varied and superlative repertoire, while the dancer might bring her desire for more frequent demi-soloist roles. Sometimes these desires mesh, but sometimes, of course, they clash.

The relationship, therefore, between the artistic director and the dancer is always changing, never static; it is fluid in the sense that each performance will carry with it demands and challenges that were not present in the prior performance. And so the artistic director and the dancer must cope with these circumstances while maintaining an effective working relationship. Knowing in advance, for instance, that they might tend to look at the same event in different ways can ease further problems down the line.

The point is to understand where the other person is coming from. Simple, really.

Yet not so simple because where the other person—especially the artistic director—comes from has been changing. Fifteen years ago dancers could expect less of a "bottom line" standard, more of a creative-artistic emphasis from artistic directors. No more, though. Balanced budgets and hype and efficient management have taken over, and dancers must understand that all of this affects performing opportunities, repertoire, even scheduling. Kennet Oberly of the Ballet Iowa puts it quite plainly: "I've seen a tremendous change in atmosphere and attitude of dance companies," he says, thinking back a couple of years to when the University of Iowa asked him to prepare a major lecture on the work of an artistic director. "I realized that when I became an artistic director, I quickly grew disappointed because when I was dancing I had seen artistic directors do the creative stuff, nothing but choreograph, letting others do the nuts and bolts. But now I saw that things had become very businesslike, and artistic directors had begun to wear many hats. . . . They must know how to fund-raise, for instance, yet fund-raising and creating a ballet are both full-time things, so what do you do? You're forced to create faster; often you're forced to rely on ready-made formulas. You look to see what ballets you can do to keep audience attendance up, to pump up ticket sales." He mentions Peter Martins of the New York City Ballet, calling him "a genius fund-raiser." He admires what Martins has been able to do with his company. "The blond hair, wearing the nice suit, offering the firm handshake," these are attributes Kennet Oberly feels make for good fund-raising, and he knows that artistic directors of the future had better understand what will be expected of them.

Because artistic directors can no longer rely on the world admiring their creative genius alone. And dancers had better understand this as well. The distance between artistic director and dancer has grown enormously. "Artistic directors' attitudes have changed," Oberly believes. "They are far more removed from the dancer now; they are more of an office, a figure, and you hear from them via someone else."

Mary Day, artistic director of the Washington (D.C.) Ballet, echoes Oberly. "To maintain the nonprofit status and raise money, that's the way the role has changed and continues to change," she says. "We're finding ourselves spending more time behind the desk and less time in the studio." It's not a spot that Mary Day, or Kennet Oberly, or most other artistic directors, wax enthusiastic over. They are, after all, dancers who spent much of their early lives performing and creating. They became dancers because they loved to dance, and when their dance careers were over, their love for the art form had hardly diminished. One thing they didn't count on, though, was that *someone* had to tame the raging beast of ballet company expenses; that someone turned out to be themselves because only they were in a position of making final decisions and understanding how all the strands of the company pulled together.

And so today artistic directors are not what dancers used to think they were: creative geniuses who could work closely with their dancers, offering understanding and hands-on support. Dancers had a "special" relationship with artistic directors based on their common training, common love for dance, and common career suffering. Dancers *knew* they were special because the artistic director had been one of them, and he or she was never going to forget that.

But no more. The artistic director may still have empathy with the dancers, may still feel the bond of common experience, but it is to the bankers and the businessmen that he or she must bow. Because without their financial support, there would be no company for the dancers, and there would be no position for the artistic director.

This doesn't mean the artistic director is or should be unreachable, simply that the job of artistic director has become more business-oriented and less dancer-involved. But good artistic directors still find time for their dancers.

Take Bruce Marks of the Boston Ballet. He estimates he spends five to six hours each week counseling dancers and answering questions such as, "Where am I going?"; "Am I going to make it?"; and "Why was I cast this way?"

Dancers' personal problems can take many forms, but there are certain vaguely defined rules about what can be brought into the studio and what should be left outside. Most artistic directors feel that a dancer's personal life, so long as it doesn't impinge on his or her dancing or conduct outside the studio, is beyond inquiry or interest. Studio life and personal life should be separate and distinct. "As a ballet master before I became an artistic director," recalls Kennet Oberly, "we were all friends; we went out and did things together. But now I'm calling the shots, and I have to hold back some. For me, the cardinal rule is that you must walk into that studio and put your personal life on the shelf."

Still, Oberly underscores what Bruce Marks has said about counseling dancers, in spite of trying to erect barriers between studio life and outside life. "You turn out to be a pop psychiatrist," he says, "because you are an authoritative figure, and the dancers come to you with problems. Certainly as a human being and on a human level, if someone comes and asks me to

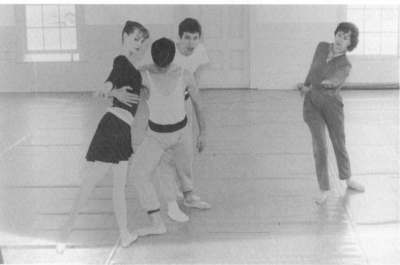

Although the role of artistic director is changing, a good artistic director will always find time to be with the dancers, and sometimes is the resident choreographer. Top: Bruce Marks with his Boston Ballet company. Bottom: Angela Whitehill with dancers of Vermont Ballet Theatre. © Ralph J. Carbo, Jr.

help them, then as a human being I will, though all I have to offer is my own personal experiences. But," he emphasizes, "if the dancers come to me, it does not affect any decision about them whatsoever in the studio or in the workplace. They come to me strictly off the record, as a human being."

For Oberly, studio time is serious time, and dancers' personal problems have only a limited place. "It's both the dancers' responsibility and the director's responsibility to treat the studio like a church. We're there to work; we're there to create something," he says. Preparing a ballet for performance takes so much pure labor that there is little time to let anything else get in the way. "You have to develop another kind of relationship in the studio," he says. "Often there are dancers I don't like, who I don't want to be with, but if they respect their own work, and I respect their work, we get along just fine in the studio, and I don't worry about what they are doing outside the studio."

But it can work the other way as well. Oberly tells the story of a dancer in his company who was going through a major personal trauma. Oberly and the dancer remained close friends outside the studio, "but inside the studio he was going through big changes in his life: he was uncertain whether he wanted to continue dancing; he had a lot of self-confidence problems." His personality turned aggressive and angry, and he grew quite violent and difficult to control. Quite obviously the dancer's personal problems had slipped into the studio and now were affecting his ability to perform. "It got to the point where the entire company was fed up with him," Oberly remembers, "when he would enter a room, a dark cloud would come over everyone." This dancer happened to be big and powerful, and Oberly needed him to finish out the season, so he—and the company—endured the disagreeableness for another few weeks. "But it was apparent he knew how crippled he was, so what we did was to stand back and let him go into a corner and try and work his problems out."

In fact, this dancer did drop out of ballet, but Oberly's surmise of the situation is a lot less final and a lot more uncertain: "As an artistic director, you are constantly confronted with people who do not keep their personal problems outside the studio, and you're constantly faced with having to push things aside."

There are circumstances, however, when an artistic director should feel that dancers' personal lives cannot be left without some attention. This is often the case with young dancers on the verge of a professional career—in their late teens—perhaps far from home and certainly in their first few months of self-support. Artistic directors who ignore the unsettledness and loneliness inherent in such a situation make it very easy for a young dancer's personal problems to multiply until they definitely will affect what goes on in the studio.

Still, there are dancers who will say, "The artistic director has no right to interfere in my personal life. Period!"

They mean it, oh how they mean it! These are times when the artistic director has to step back and assess the dancer, ask a few pertinent questions such as, "Have you ever lived away from home before?"; "Are you getting proper rest and are you eating well?"; "Do you keep in touch with your family on a regular basis?"; "Are you having boy/girlfriend problems?"; "Financial problems?"; "Do you feel casting is unfair?"

If the answers soothe him, then, perhaps, he can step away from the dancer's personal life.

Sometimes not, though. Take Richard Englund, artistic director of Joffrey II. In his position he works with many, many young dancers, and he considers it his responsibility to stay involved in his dancers' lives. "We're a transition company," he says, "and when the dancers are very young [in their late teens] we have a responsibility to know they are not in danger or in extremely awkward circumstances." What he means, of course, is that his company dancers are at the edge of a professional career, and they are of an age where they still need some looking after. Even so, Englund tries to avoid prying or otherwise complicating the dancers' lives. "When problems do arise," he says, "we have to inquire and try to find out what's going on without the dancer feeling we are being too nosy." He sees the dancer not only as the instrument of the director but as an artist in his or her own right, and this, he feels, can create major difficulties if not handled properly. "The instrument and the artist within the same person is so fraught with problems that dancers should never feel they have been neglected or controlled."

Thus, some hands-on concern but not too much agenda-making.

And it's only for a limited period. "By the time they are in a full company, and theoretically self-supporting, pushing into their midtwenties, their personal lives really shouldn't be our concern."

Perhaps the most ongoing uncertainty in the continually changing relationship between artistic director and dancer is what many call "attitude"—the way artistic directors and dancers approach their art, the feelings they engender about their work, and the way they accomplish what they set out to do. Make no mistake, "attitude" is a force that *both* artistic directors and dancers must cope with. Both have it; both can misuse it; both can destroy themselves with it.

You think artistic directors can't have an "attitude" problem? Take this story Janelle tells about her director and the ballet company they both worked for. "We were doing a premier that involved some acting and some dance, and we had to work on a huge platform. It had two wide panels and four stairs, a Greek set with big pillars. We worked in the studio, pretending where these things were, but the choreography really depended on their exact location and it just wasn't the same. The artistic director simply blocked his mind; he wasn't open to any suggestions about how the choreography might need to be changed. Then we got in the theatre, and we spent an entire week rearranging things that could have been anticipated beforehand and allowed for in the studio."

A waste of time, she says, a waste of talent. It could have been avoided so easily, but "he was an artistic director who got an idea in his mind and was very resistant to any changes at all."

Attitude. Artistic director attitude.

Then there's the other side . . . dancer attitude. "Attitude has always affected me very deeply," retorts Mary Day of the Washington Ballet. "More than it should probably, but I can't help that it's the way I am. If I find we have anybody with 'attitude,' we try to get them out right away because I think that they can infect the entire organization."

What, exactly, is attitude, then? It's a measure of dissatisfaction with your current position and prospects, something that causes you to speak out and develop conflicts within the company. It can be a lack of a sense of cooperation or a meanness when dealing with others' feelings or an inability to take even the mildest constructive criticism. It is divisive, and it singles you out in uncomplimentary terms.

A reputation for "attitude" will follow you throughout your career. The reason? Artistic directors talk to one another regularly; they consult over new dancers, new works, new approaches. They also check out résumé matter, and all it takes is a simple phone call to one of your former artistic directors, and your reputation will have followed along.

You avoid such a reputation by keeping your dissatisfaction to yourself, by remaining pleasant and cooperative (even though you may be planning furiously for a flood of auditions to get you out of this awful company), and by fulfilling the terms of your contract. Don't follow the lead of Terri who walked out in the middle of the season because "I wasn't giving enough to the company." She felt they couldn't give her enough either, that the entire process was not working. "I felt it was best to leave," she says, knowing it was unprofessional, but leaving anyway. "The artistic director thought I should have stuck it out and stayed with her company, and in the course of our last conversation she told me I was not a dancer and never would be."

Terri's face grows somber. "I remember that conversation as the worst experience I ever had."

Attitude. It almost destroyed Terri's career. She's dancing now, doing well, but the chances of her walking out on another contract are small indeed.

When we speak of "attitude" we tend to think only of its negative aspects, though there really can be a positive side as well. Sometimes a *good* attitude can make a major difference. Mary Day, for example, has a story to tell. "Recently, I had a lengthy conversation with one of our male dancers who is adequate but never going to be a cavalier." The trouble was that he *wanted* to be a cavalier, had his heart set on it, and had trained religiously for years. But Mary Day concluded his talents lay in another direction. "He is very good in jazz," she says, "and in modern and tap dancing. He sings and plays the guitar, and he could make his way in musicals. He even has family contacts in the film industry." He can do all sorts of things in the theatre, she believed, and she talked to him about it, offering him alternatives. "I tried to make him face reality," she says, "because he is never going to be a classic cavalier."

Never?

"Never! You say, 'Look, we have got to find the niche where you can best achieve.' "

A good attitude makes it happen.

The very nature of the relationship between artistic director and dancer—close, instructive, interdependent—makes it apparent there should be some role call of responsibilities running between them. Each must owe the other something, each should expect something from the other in return—otherwise the relationship has no connection. It would be like two vehicles, one Ford, one Cadillac, moving down parallel highway lanes, side by side, unaware that one is about to cross into the other's lane. Without signals, without *communication*, chaos—or worse—would develop.

The same is true in a ballet company. Artistic director and dancers must interconnect; they must have some confidence about what will be expected of them and what they can expect. Some might call it a young performer's bill of rights and obligations, but the truth is that it is simply the code by which the young professional dancer lives.

What, then, can the dancer expect from the artistic director?
• a comfortable, safe place to work

• challenging, eclectic choreography

• a reasonable working period and realistic rehearsal hours

• respect for his or her talent

• acknowledgment of accomplishments

• a friendly ear when problems arise

• a well-run company

By the same token, what does the dancer *owe* to the artistic director?
• understanding of and adherence to the rules of the company

• prompt attendance in daily class

• working to his or her highest ability

• knowledge of how to pace oneself

• keeping personal problems out of the studio

• a positive attitude

• understanding casting decisions

• conducting oneself professionally in and out of the theatre and studios

Above all else you should remember this: as with any other job, yours is part of a larger entity. It's a business, and in that respect it's not much different from any other business or corporation. It may be called a "company," but it is really a business, even if the bottom line at the end of the fiscal year wavers a bit.

"Business!" you exclaim. "I'm an artist."

In ballet, you'll find out, the two work hand in hand.

Ask any artistic director.

CASTING

> *Often, it's the squeaky wheel that gets the part.*
> —*Martine van Hamel, prima ballerina,*
> *American Ballet Theatre*

"I knew she'd get that role!"
"You never know what he's looking for!"
"She asked to audition, she almost begged . . . "

Just as reactions vary as to who is cast in what role, so the nature of the casting process varies from company to company. Some make it pretty clear by putting together a corps de ballet that follows a certain consistency of height, weight, even hair color. Others offer few external clues, yet establish their needs by emphasizing physical varieties among the dancers themselves. The point is that the casting process is quite personal to the individual company and artistic director. You, the young dancer, have to understand that what might seem appropriate in one company may have little relevance in another.

For example, if your company dances the classics a great deal *(Swan Lake, Giselle, Sleeping Beauty, Paquita),* the artistic director will probably choose his corps de ballet for height, body type, and similarity of looks. The corps members must be mirror images of one another because that is the classical style. Thus, if you are blonde, five-foot three, fair skinned, and muscular, your chances of joining a company of five-foot six dancers, slender formed with dark hair, are small. In the classical tradition, uniformity is key, and your blonde looks and muscular body type would stand out when they shouldn't.

This uniformity can go beyond the company level. It may seem difficult to believe but from about 1930 through the late 1960s, in Europe, dancers needed to be brunette; anything else—blonde, red haired, or any variation—did not measure up to the traditional "ballerina" look. If you wanted a job, if you wanted to dance and remain employed, you had better be a brunette.

It didn't mean that brunettes danced better than blondes or redheads, just that tradition demanded this type of selection. Company after company conformed until an entire continent presented itself as the image of uniformity.

It can even go further than the way you look. In Diaghelev's Ballet Russe de Monte Carlo, uniformity extended to the name you used. It was important to emphasize the *Russian* nature of the company, so . . . Alicia Marks became Alicia Markova, Sidney Patrick Chipendall Healey-Kay became Anton Dolin, and so forth.

It is important to realize that classical ballet in its most traditional form embodies the art of conformity; the beauty and the grace come because dancers do the same thing together, at the same time, and with the same effect. Take a look at video recordings of the Kirov Ballet's *La Bayadère* or *Swan Lake.* Note how the dancers in the lines are all doing the same step at

Here is an ingenue part danced fittingly by a young performer. Albert Volk and Kim Nichol in Death and the Maiden. © Ralph J. Carbo, Jr.

the same time in the same costume with the same hair and makeup . . . even their shoes have the same patina!

No one can deny there is beauty in this vivid conformity. At the same time, though, it must be understood that this conformity is based upon a selection process. A six-foot dancer, for instance, will hardly fit the role of Puck in *Midsummer Night's Dream,* and a five-foot three-inch male will certainly not be appropriate to dance cavalier and prince roles opposite taller females. The point is that to understand the casting process you have to realize it is made up partly of conformity, partly of selection, both working together to provide a company "persona" which can then be translated into a certain company style.

It's pretty obvious that contemporary dance standards are less rigid than those the classics require, the idea of uniformity becoming less important than individual sparkle or "expression." And sometimes, in this modern world, a company has to be prepared to go both ways—modern as well as classical. Take the Hartford (Conn.) Ballet, for example. Artistic Director Michael Uthoff often chooses ballets incorporating his own contemporary style. But he also leans toward classics such as *Nutcracker* and *Coppélia* as well as such neoclassical works as Balanchine's *Concerto Barocco* and *Allegro Brilliante* . . . and even an occasional work by ultramodern Pilobolus!

A wide range indeed!

And there's no way he can apply the classical approach to uniformity in this diverse repertoire. So he has some female dancers who are five-foot nine and ten, others who are only five-foot three; he has a male who is

In contemporary dance, the idea of uniformity becomes less important than individual expression. Dancers of Eddy Toussaint de Montreal. © Giancarlo Manzoni.

barely five-foot four, and another who is over six feet. This allows Uthoff the freedom to maintain a wide repertoire and to offer substantial casting opportunities.

Here's what Melissa Sondrini, one of his dancers, says: "Michael casts two dancers for each part; he never posts a cast list until he's sure he has the right choice, and he's very supportive of dancers understudying any role." Uthoff allows his dancers to learn any part they wish, so long as they don't get in the way of the first cast, and he frequently allows understudies to dance the roles in performance. Sondrini remembers when it happened to her. "I was an apprentice and cast as an understudy to 'friends' in *Coppélia,* and one of the dancers became injured. It was the end of the season, the last set of performances before contract talks. So I went on for the entire run, and I think it secured my position with the company. I know it helped Michael to make the decision to give me soloist and principal roles."

No young dancer should be uncertain about her or his strengths or casting points. You must understand how—and when—type casting plays a part in the role you get. Are you a tall, willowy dancer who looks best being promenaded in an arabesque penchée? Are you the strong powerhouse with the flashing black eyes who executes à la seconde turns with a Latin flair? Or are you the romantic poet or Prince Albrecht? Is your forte partnering? Turning? Jumping? Are you romantic and sensuous?

Are you, in essence, classical, contemporary, or jazz oriented? There's only one rule here, and it's quite simple: *KNOW YOUR STRENGTHS AND DEVELOP THEM!* Don't yearn for a part for which you could never be suited; understand yourself and your limitations.

KNOW YOUR STRENGTHS AND DEVELOP THEM!

Artistic directors all pay homage to this rule. They see you as a bundle of strengths and weaknesses, and they strive to project you and your strengths while concealing your weaknesses. They cast you according to your strengths.

Or think of Eddy Toussaint and his Ballet de Montréal. The company is known for choreography with a contemporary flavor, but recently Toussaint decided to present an all new version of *Nutcracker.* The ballet was set in outer space, but Toussaint wanted to include a traditional "Snow Scene," and so he chose his Snow Queen for her pure classical line and training. A month into rehearsals this dancer fell ill, and her understudy assumed the part. But the understudy—while similar in body type to the ill dancer—had much more contemporary training and much less classical training. "I never felt quite right in the part," the understudy said, reflecting on the experience. "I'm just not that suited to traditional, classical style." It could have had a much less happy ending than it did—the original dancer recovered just in time to dance the part on opening night.

For the understudy there were no tears, no recriminations—only relief that she had been spared what would have been a poor dance experience.

It's one thing to understand how the casting eye of your artistic director works. It's quite something else to have a new choreographer walk into the studio to set a new work or restage an old one. By now you should be familiar with your artistic director's peculiar leanings (always understanding, of course, that artistic directors will seek to find and emphasize a dancer's strengths above all else), but here is someone new, and a few of your assumptions may have to be reformed.

The one thing you can be sure about is that when this new choreographer casts the work, he or she will be searching for strengths and weaknesses in the dancers. Remember, the choreographer doesn't know any more about you than you do about him or her, so you must project yourself to give effect to what you do best. Be sure you are in the front line when he asks you to do petit allégro, if that's your forte, or if your extension is high, that you are wearing the best tights to show off your lovely legs.

Usually, at the outset, the artistic director and the ballet master consult with the choreographer and offer casting suggestions based on the position of the dancer in the company. If you're a principal, if you're a soloist, if you're a member of the corps, these ranks will weigh upon your ultimate casting. But there are other considerations the new choreographer will seek to uncover about each dancer. They will come out in consultation with the artistic director and ballet master. Such considerations include:

• your work habits

• your facility to learn

• your dancer type (allégro, adagio, contemporary, classical, romantic, soubrette, etc.)

• your body configuration (tall, short, willowy, compact)

The choreographer's next step is to watch class. If in your company apprentices and company members take separate classes, this could be a problem because the choreographer will undoubtedly be under time pressure, and he or she may simply not be able to attend both sets of classes all the way through. What you should hope for—as an apprentice—is that the choreographer will see the separate classes on separate days or will attend at least a portion of each class.

We assume, then, that you will be seen and that the choreographer will make his choices after the classes end. *But note:* the choreographer, after class and after you have been chosen, will probably ask you to execute some of the steps or lifts from the new ballet. This is a final test, a mini-audition, to be sure he or she has chosen wisely. It is simply an insurance policy.

But of course you'll perform brilliantly, won't you?

Suppose, though, you don't impress the new choreographer sufficiently to land a role in the new ballet. All is not lost; a new opportunity might become available. Because a new ballet often uses the company principals and soloists, it monopolizes their time and efforts, leaving open spots in some of the company's older works. Where does the artistic director look?

To the corps, of course, many of whom have been understudying these roles right along. Suddenly you will be dancing the part in performance or you will be cast in a major role that requires substantial rehearsal. Either way, you have been elevated from the corps, and your opportunity to present a true picture of your talent has come. Now it's up to you to make the most of it.

So, the appearance of a new choreographer setting a new work should fill you with anticipation, regardless of whether you are chosen to dance in it. It is a time of opportunity, and you should approach it positively and with confidence. Something good is sure to happen!

Believe it or not, even that annual extravaganza, *Nutcracker,* can provide a new casting opportunity. It can move you from the corps to a soloist role in one easy step. Most companies, as you know, use two or three casts in this Christmas favorite, and a young hopeful is often tapped to dance a variation in the second act, especially when the company is on tour or providing an early morning children's program. This accomplishes two things: the artistic director can evaluate the young hopeful (it could be you) and at the same time provide a regular cast member a needed break. Professional companies dance as many as fifty performances of this classic between Thanksgiving and Christmas, sometimes two or three perform-ances a day, so this is the time when opportunity beckons. Casting decisions cannot be so rigid with this difficult schedule; there must be some flexibility and change. Who benefits? The dancer who is ready for a new challenge, who wants to move out of the corps and into a soloist role.

Could that dancer be you?

But beware the fragile-ego syndrome, the conviction that once you have danced a part it is yours forever. Nothing works this way in the ballet world.

Nothing.

Bruce Marks, artistic director of the Boston Ballet, explains by way of example: "Not long ago one of my principal dancers came in because she had not been cast as the lead in a big, big ballet we were doing. 'It's like a slap in the face,' she said. I asked her two questions: 'Who danced the lead on opening night last year in this ballet?' 'I did,' she admitted. 'What position did you have in this company before I cast you as the lead?' 'I was a soloist,' she answered. 'See,' I said, 'this role made you a principal; now it's time for someone else.' "

Did she understand?

"She understood." Bruce Marks smiles.

And that is the nature of the casting process. It is neither so cut and dried as to be relegated to a mathematical formula, nor so impractical as to be controlled by whim and impulse. There is logic in the casting process, yet all is tempered by a sense of what will seem right, what will show well. People are cast by their physical proportions, but this is not the only reason they are cast in a role. Somehow, the artistic director and the choreographer must juggle talent and technique along with physical projection in order to present an integrated whole. It is not an easy task, but when the right casting decisions have been made, it is as apparent as the snug fit of a ballet shoe.

And you will feel it too!

THE COSTUMER

> *I often think the greatest influence towards design came in the nineteenth century from two Frenchmen, Msrs. Maillot and Jules Leotard when they gave us tights and leotards which to this day have become the traditional clothes for dancers world wide.*
>
> —*Dame Alicia Markova,*
> *British prima ballerina*

The costume shop, that strangely beguiling somewhat mysterious designation, is a ballet company's most formidable off-stage location. Magic is brewed here: colors and fabrics are fused; whole transformations occur. This is where the world of ballet and the world of illusion come together, where the dancer's art and the costumer's creations forge a bond so the audience *wants* to believe. This is where reality becomes performance and dancer becomes character, and where what one wears is the symbol of who one is, at least on stage.

Here's a typical costume shop: windows rise from floor to ceiling. A low wooden counter runs across them at waist level, with several open bins underneath. Each is marked by a different color slash for the particular fabric to be stored there: red, blue, green, and so forth.

Along another wall is a group of old black sewing machines, each operated by a seamstress, while on the opposite wall hang pages of drawings, swatches of material, rulers, and shelves with paints and paint brushes. In the middle of the room stands a drafting table on which the company costumer is working out new designs. Chances are this costumer is a former dancer, likely to be in her early- to mid-forties and quite adept at her work.

Against a fourth wall several large wooden crates on wheels stand, with doors opened and costumes hung over the sides. These are "road boxes," and they follow the company on tour. They carry all the costumes, shoes, headdresses, irons, steamers, and sewing paraphernalia needed to conjure a regular stream of costume-shop magic. Without them dancers would simply become dancers again, and the illusion would fall away.

Shoes, too, play an important part inside the costume shop. What's a proper costume without the proper shoes; can the illusion survive if the lovely costume is made ordinary by unlovely shoes? Costumers know this. They understand what someone like Teresina Goheen, a soloist with the Tulsa, Oklahoma Ballet, might feel: "I've always had problems with shoes because I've never been able to wear stock shoes until recently. None of them lasts long enough; by the time you break them in, they are too soft, and they just don't work."

The costume shop has the answer, and in a nearby storage room there is box upon box, row upon row of shoes, with a dancer's name firmly affixed to each carton. It's important to keep the dancers happy, so the costumers make sure the *right* kind of shoes are there.

But the dancers need to do their part too. A soloist, for example, knows she will be allotted about 100–150 pairs of shoes a season, and certainly that seems a substantial supply. Yet young dancers must come to understand how quickly shoes can be used up, and what seemed such an inexhaustible supply at the beginning of the season can become barely sufficient by the last few weeks. Any seasoned professional will tell you, *"Be careful with your shoes!"* Use old ones for rehearsals, make every effort to shellac them, and make them last as long as possible.

The costumer wants to help, but the company budget can be an unforgiving monster.

Suppose you're a principal dancer with your company, and you're coming in for a costume fitting. You've dried yourself thoroughly so no perspiration will cling to the newly designed material. At a signal you follow the costumer to a screened-off portion of the shop.

"We'll do the bodice, first," the costumer might say, picking up a multisectioned garment with hooks and eyes attached to the back.

The costume is lovely, of course, but you wonder why bodices in ballet costumes have so many sections.

"All those seams give you more places to breathe and allow you to expand your lungs," the costumer answers. "It also gives us more opportunity to make adjustments as your body changes or as other dancers might need to use the costume."

The costumer could then pin a long piece of velvet piping around the top, and she might ask whether you would like the front cut low. "I'll put souffle in it, a special flesh-colored fabric that stretches with you," she might add. "You can't fall out and it can't be seen, even from the wings."

Next comes the tutu, and here is where the costumer's work takes time. The simplest tutu often takes up to twenty hours to make. According to Pat Pickette of London's Royal Ballet, where the costume department occupies three floors, "Our fastest workers can do one in about fourteen hours, but the average is longer." Tutus are such personalized things; no two are quite alike, and the costumer has to tack it by hand, using heavy thread, so the tutu can lie flat, so the light can get beneath it and show off the dancer's lovely legs.

When the costumer is finished, you still have work to do. Now you will want to check the supply of *your* pointe shoes, the ones tucked away with your special lot and size number. A new costume should always cause you to do this because it means you will be facing a lengthy series of new performances, and the supply of pointe shoes had better be sufficient. With some contemporary companies, in fact, *all* the shoes, including pointe shoes, are dyed to match the costumes, and your shoes could shrink because of this. The costumer will know whether this will happen, and you should be prepared to adjust your size accordingly. (In Ballet de Montréal, for example, all the dancers are required to use cotton ribbon with their pointe shoes because it takes the dye more easily *and* the material is softer on the Achilles tendon, but the shoes still can shrink.)

Shoes, of course, are one of a young dancer's most important tools.

Costumes and ballet shoes are highly important, personalized items supplied by a company for performers. Left: © Patricia Brain; right: © Terry L. Spilken, courtesy *The Dancer's Foot Book* (available from Princeton Book Company).

Through the years you have developed your own needs concerning style and brand, but even so, you have added your own special, personal adjustments, and you've communicated them to the shoe manufacturer so that the pointe shoes have been delivered exactly as you've wished them. They are exactly right.

But beware!

The dancer with special orders—even the smallest changes in a stock shoe—can find herself waiting from three to six months for delivery, especially if the shoes are to be delivered from outside the United States.

What kinds of special adjustments could cause delays that might even render you shoeless? There's the "dorsey cut" that lowers the side of the shoe, giving the illusion of a better arch, the one-half or three-quarter shank shoe, the high vamp, the low vamp, the raised heel or shortened box, the one-quarter size variation. All of these apparently "simple" adjustments are really not so simple in execution, and a shoe manufacturer might well put special orders for these adjustments on the bottom of the order pile.

Sybil, a young dancer with a western company, describes what she went through to get what she felt was the proper shoe. In the process she learned that special ordering a new shoe was not the same as asking for special ingredients in a delicatessen order. "I don't think the company ever realized how much time and energy was involved," Sybil remembers. "It would take an hour to get to the factory, at least an hour trying on and testing the new shoes, and another hour to get home. True, I finally have a shoe that works for me, but now the shoe company is using a new factory, and we have to start the whole process again. And my feet suffer until the shoes are right!"

What to do, then, if you are having a problem with your shoes? One thing to be wary about is the local shoe supplier. Chances are these people, willing though they might be, know little about the care and fit of a young professional dancer's foot, and your problems could be magnified with the wrong advice or treatment. It's worth a special trip to New York City when you're on layoff or to the shoe manufacturer's headquarters to establish what's right for you.

And the right shoe this year may not be the same shoe you wear throughout your dancing life. Local shoe suppliers probably don't know this, but shoe manufacturers do. Your needs change as your dancing changes, and you want to be in a position to acquire the best shoe for your dance needs at all times.

Some shoes bear a "maker's" insignia on the sole, a trademark really, but dancers sometimes come to think of this as a talisman for their dancing, a type of good luck symbol, and they grow dependent on one shoe manufacturer.

"I can't dance well in any other shoe!" young dancers will wail when they find themselves forced to use another maker. "I feel so awkward; it just doesn't work right."

Such loyalty might have its place in other contexts, but with pointe shoes the reality of the business marketplace is more certain. Shoe manufacturers come and go. Trademarks are passed on to other shoe manufacturers; some are redesigned or shifted to other products. Insignias, which are usually personal to the individual cobbler, do not always remain with that cobbler. The point is this: the trademark or insignia of a shoe manufacturer is no different than any other asset in that business; it can be sold, bought, changed, phased out, or reapplied. Linking good fortune to such an unreliable talisman can only bring disappointment.

In general, men are much luckier when it comes to shoes. They are easier to fit, and their dancing is not as demanding on shoes because, of course, they do no pointe work. So the number of shoes a male dancer needs depends on his costumes since ballet aesthetics demand that his shoes match his tights to extend the line of the leg. What's the most preferred men's shoe material? Canvas, probably, because it can be more easily dyed to match costumes.

The costume shop and the costumer bring the magic of ballet into focus for the dancer because it is here that the illusion of beauty and grace is first developed. From shoes, to tights, to tutus, to headdresses, the dancer's character is created, and in a very real sense it is the costumer who holds power over your performance.

The costumer, in fact, can be one of your best friends. Just moving the skirt of a tutu up or down one-half inch will make your legs look long and slender or short and dumpy; other adjustments can make your waist look wide or your hips bulky.

Trust your costumer! Key words, important advice. Remember that having your interest at heart is the way the costumer keeps the job. Costuming is an art too. Young dancers who keep a running argument going with costumers may find themselves with a reputation within the company for being *difficult!*

Costumers and their sensibilities should not be taken lightly. There is the story of a well-known New York costumer who was so hassled by the artistic director of a national company and his dancers that she took an entire set of newly designed costumes and threw them into the path of a speeding taxi.

Or the tale of a prima ballerina who insisted that her tutu skirt be lower than those of the corps, so the costumer quietly dropped the skirt an extra one-half inch beyond the original fit. The dancer's legs lost all shape while the legs of the corps' dancers sparkled with grace and beauty.

All of this settles down to one major principle, and young dancers should commit it to memory: *costumers know best about costumes; trust their artistry.* If you want to make costume changes, speak to the costumer or the wardrobe mistress, but never, ever, make changes on your own.

And remember, the costumer is in charge of costumes, all costumes, even yours. Tim Miano, a dancer with the Dayton Ballet, recalls how one year the shifting visions of the costumer changed the effect of a performance from night to night. "We'd have another piece of equipment to put on each evening. The first night we had a plain leotard, the next night we had some lapels, then we had ribbing across the chest, then cuffs, then buttons on our cuffs . . . and by the seventh performance we had become completely dressed." He adds, with some admiration, that such constant change meant the costumers were sewing each evening and fitting dancers every day. "They finally got it right, halfway through the engagement."

But it was the costumers who made the decisions, and the costumers who took the responsibility. In fact, young dancers should never assume costume responsibility for themselves. *The costumer knows best about costumes,* and if any problems with costumes require contact with the artistic director, it is best to let the costumer take it up with him or her directly.

Don't get in the middle!

Heed this story from a retired national-company dancer who almost made such a mistake. "We had a well-known choreographer setting a piece on the company," she remembers, "and he demanded specially designed and dyed leotards. We were on tour in Washington state, and the wardrobe mistress only took the costumes to be washed once a week because the dying was so delicate." She grimaces. "I was horrified because I had lots of lifts which brought me close to my partner again and again, so I pleaded to take my costume to the motel where I could wash it myself. Reluctantly, she agreed, but after washing the costume in the evening, I found it didn't dry out by morning. So I turned on the oven and popped the costume in for a couple of minutes while I brushed my teeth. When I opened the oven door, I found to my horror, not a leotard but a handful of melted nylon!" She laughs. "I went to the wardrobe mistress and told her I would confess to the artistic director, but she wouldn't allow it. 'I will do it!' she said, and she marched right out and took the blame."

It was her responsibility, you see, and it wasn't the dancer's place to jump in the middle.

Costumes do need special attention; they must be treated with consideration and foresight. Every young dancer must be careful not to:

• sit in a costume

• eat or drink in a costume

• smoke in a costume (Although fabrics are treated so they won't go up in flames, every so often it happens, in spite of all the assurances.)

• throw a costume on the floor

• leave a costume unattended, once a quick change has been made (Hand it to your dresser or ask one of the other dancers to return it to the dressing room and hang it up.)

And remember, *the costumer knows best about costumes!*

THE ADMINISTRATIVE STAFF

The dancer has to be prepared to do interviews, social
events, and be a public representative off stage.
—Ken Hertz, former general administrator,
Atlanta Ballet

Dancers do not live by dance alone! This adage, familiar and timely, is never
more true than when you need a pair of house seats in a hurry . . . or when
you *must* have a stock photo to send to Cousin Harriet on her one
hundredth birthday! . . . or when you want the name of a reputable—and
inexpensive—financial adviser because the income tax filing deadline is but
a week away!

There are many people in a dance company who don't dance, yet they
are, in their own way, as important to you as your ballet master. Never
forget that the company is made up of those with artistic responsibilities as
well as those with nonartistic responsibilities; both must function well if
the company is to succeed.

For you the key is to understand and to get along. Understand why the
company needs nonartistic staff; get along with them because the
company—and thus, you—stand to benefit.

Ballet veterans have little appreciation for the young dancer who arrives
with an overweening sense of self-importance and proceeds to insult,
belittle, and behave with queenly indifference toward the nonartistic staff.
The dancer is but one of the spokes in the ballet wheel, important to be
sure, but not so important that others pale by comparison. The nonartistic
staff can be the young dancer's best friend . . . or most implacable foe.

The direction is pretty much up to you.

At the top of the nonartistic staff list is the company general manager.
He or she is in charge of all nonartistic personnel, and your chances of
having much contact are fairly slim. Simply put, your paths will rarely cross
because in the company you do little with which the general manager is
concerned. This doesn't mean, of course, that the general manager is not
important to you—anyone with these responsibilities *has* to be important
to a dancer. But there are too many layers of administrative hierarchy
between you and the general manager for there to be much contact.

You will, however, see the general manager if financial issues arise and a
company meeting is called. He or she may discuss such items as raises
(imagine a smiling general manager!), or decreases in salaries (imagine an
embattled general manager!), changes in contracted weeks, changes in

health insurance premiums or coverage, perhaps the logistics of an upcoming tour. Even here, though, your contact with the general manager will be on a group basis; rarely will you be sitting down one on one.

That is, until you become a principal dancer. Then, many things change. You are now on a level of importance that allows your ideas, thoughts, wishes, even demands to be taken seriously by the highest level of nonartistic personnel—the general manager. But for you, the young dancer, your level of importance within the company circle remains relatively low, and your needs can be more than adequately met by someone below the general manager.

Ken Hertz, general manager of the Atlanta Ballet, is pleased when a young dancer seeks him out for no other reason than to be friendly, though he sees it in strictly generalized terms. "I think it's nice for the dancers to get to know the administrative staff," he says, "but it's really not important." What he means is that such friendliness does not affect the way he does his job, nor does it change the way things are run. But it's not without its redeeming aspects. "It does help," he adds, "to create a family feeling," and this makes the company more cohesive and positive.

At least such friendliness can mean that war between artistic and nonartistic staff can be lined out. A "family feeling" is what every young dancer should strive for.

Ken Hertz doesn't dismiss young dancers out of hand simply because they aren't important to the way he does his job. "I try to get to know the dancers after the performances," he says. From time to time his acquaintances among the dancers prove useful: a board member might wish an introduction or a table of volunteers might wish to learn more about the dancer's art. To nonartistic outsiders, Ken Hertz is the ultimate nonartistic insider, and he is of more benefit to the company if he can bring dancers together with nonartistic outsiders and thereby bridge a gap of curiosity.

"Dancers need to be available and adaptable," he believes, even though he will rarely need you.

The one nonartistic individual who will be a part of your daily world is the company manager. In fact, you will have your first contact with the company manager long before you step your well-trained toes onto the studio floor. He is the person who sends your contract. He is the one who provides you with information about your new company and home— length of season, repertory, where and how to find safe, affordable housing, who to see, when and why.

He's an apt financial answer-man too. What if . . . you've been working for two whole weeks, and the company manager walks into the studio just as rehearsal is finishing. He carries a handful of envelopes—your first paycheck! You open the envelope, right there, right then! Puzzlement strikes . . . you look at the amount; it's less—quite a bit less—than you expected.

A mistake, you think. So you ask one of the dancers:

"Who knows? I can hardly balance a checkbook!"

You ask the ballet master:

"I avoid the financial side, love."

You go to the artistic director:

"I suggest you read your contract again."

No one knows until . . . you get in touch with the company manager. *He'll* know, you can count on it! Taxes or Social Security withholding, union dues or health insurance, whatever the reason he'll be able to tell you. It's his job to know these things because the nonartistic day-to-day affairs of the company and each dancer are his responsibility.

You're about to go on tour—your first time—and you have questions, simple questions, but important to you.

Ask away:

• "Which bus do I get on?"

• "Can we get food between spacing and performance?"

• Which restaurants are open after 11:00 P.M.?"

• Should we take something to eat on the bus, or will there be stops?"

The company manager will have the answers.

• "What about per diem?"

The company manager has it, usually in cash, and he'll dispense it to you. He'll also tell you whether you must obtain a receipt, and how much—if any—is taxable.

On a day-to-day basis you will probably deal with the company manager more frequently than any other nonartistic staff member. Whenever paperwork involving you and the company comes along—whether it's your contract or health or workman's compensation forms—the company manager is the one who has the answers. He or she is important to you in so many ways, and the value of this friendship can go a long way to enhancing the benefits of your company experience. If you get along with the company manager, you will probably enjoy the company. If you have problems with the company manager, you will have a difficult company experience.

The company manager, however, doesn't shepherd you through the performance. Once you are on stage, the stage manager takes over your concerns, and the company manager turns to a relationship with the presenter or producer, collecting the company's fees and making all the "front of the house" arrangements. The stage manager handles the many backstage details that involve you and the other dancers during performance.

Once the show is over, however, the company manager resumes his relationship with you while the stage manager remains with the crew, overseeing the packing and transportation of sets and costumes. The stage manager and crew then leave immediately: they plan to arrive at the next performance location at least eight hours before you arrive so things can be set up properly.

The stage manager, then, is clearly important to you because your concerns are his concerns, at least part of the time. He may not be as ever-present as the company manager, but while you are in the theatre, and especially while you are backstage, he should have your close attention. A good stage manager is a valued friend and ally. A good stage manager puts yours and the company's interests ahead of his own, as this recollection by Taffy Waters shows:

> When I was with the Winnepeg Ballet, we had finished a performance on a Friday night and were heading for Newfoundland. It had begun to snow, and by the next morning the highways were closed. It happened that the brother of the company manager was head of the Royal Mounted Police, and we had called ahead to a truck stop to flag down the company bus which had started an hour earlier than we did. We got hold of the company manager on the bus, and he tried to get through to his brother.
>
> In the meantime we kept going, talking our way through police barricades and explaining who we were and where we were going. As we got to the outskirts of the town in Newfoundland where we were to perform, we found the police chasing us, their lights flashing. But we kept going, expecting at any moment to be met by a massive barricade and some angry Mounties. The police chased us through the town and into the school yard where we were to park, but at least we had made it!

All around us the police pulled up, by now their sirens going. When they stepped from their cars, we could see they were really annoyed, and we didn't know what to expect.

What surprise, then, when the first Mountie gets to us and peers in, saying, "Next time you need a police escort, let us go in front!"

It seems they had been prepared to escort us into the city, ordered to do so by the company manager's brother.

What they didn't expect was to have to try and catch us!

And, of course, the show did go on as planned that evening.

As you look over the company organizational chart, one department should leap out—the office of public relations. A friendly attitude is what you strive for when dealing with this office because nowhere in the company are there people with more interest in pushing you and your career forward. Most major ballet companies have public relations people on staff because the need for these services is extensive and ongoing throughout the season. Smaller companies may hire outside public relations contractors on an event-by-event basis or the artistic director may perform the public relations function.

But there's no denying the importance of this function within the company. (A New England artistic director said recently, "Dancing in a company with no public relations department is like dancing on stage with no lights.") These are the people who communicate to the general public what the company does, plans to do, or has done; these are the people who manage media relations on behalf of the company and each individual dancer; these are the people who promote and publicize you. The point to remember is this: the public relations department works for the benefit of the company as a whole, not in the narrow self-interest of any particular dancer. If the company can benefit by promoting you in a certain ballet role, so be it. If the company can benefit by profiling you because you overcame hardship or injury and continued dancing, so be it. If the company can benefit by having you appear on television interviews, so be it.

The fact that you might also benefit is incidental. It's the company that the public relations people work for. What you should reach for is that what benefits the company also benefits you. Make your interests and the interests of the company identical.

Within days after you join the company the public relations department will hand you a form that asks for information about your training, previous companies with which you have performed, roles you have danced, scholarships and awards you have received, your home address and local newspaper. The department wants to create a biography on you which can be referenced easily and quickly, should someone come seeking information or should a new company brochure be made up. It's important that you complete this form because without the information a company cannot promote you properly, and if the information is lacking, you might somehow be left out of the program or brochure.

A dancer without a bio is a dancer without a name. No one, of course, wants that to happen.

Lest you doubt the value of the public relations people, try this scenario: your company is to premiere an all new version of *Giselle*—new scenery, new costumes, and new choreography set by a well-known female ballet star. Press releases have gone out highlighting the history of the ballet, the prominence of the choreographer, the technique and brilliance of the dancers performing the roles of Giselle and Albrecht, the creativity of the costume designer. Newspaper, television, and radio interviews have gone on for weeks; the marketplace has become saturated with news of the performance.

A week before opening night, the soloist dancing Myrta, Queen of the Wilis, falls and is injured, and her understudy has come down with appendicitis. You mention you danced the role when you were a student . . . presto! You get the part.

The public relations people are ecstatic; they have a story to promote: "Young Dancer Saves Day!" The local media are contacted; a press release is prepared; your hometown newspaper is sent a copy.

The first-night audience bulges with curiosity. How will you dance, what do you look like, can you do the role? After the performance (which, of course, is a smash!) the public relations people introduce you to the critics (who have their own level of curiosity), the board of directors (who certainly want to meet the dancer who saved the performance!), the volunteers (who want to meet a genuine heroine). The next time the company performs, the audience will be searching for you, regardless of whether you are still dancing Myrta. You are no longer just a face in the crowded corps de ballet. You have acquired individuality; you are a personality.

And on that happy day when you perform another soloist role before that same audience, there will be whispers and nods: "I saw her when . . . she saved the performance!"

You couldn't have done it without the public relations department. In this case what benefited you also benefited the company.

Have you ever wondered what the development department does? Most large ballet companies have at least one person who performs this function; in smaller companies it might be assumed by the artistic director or general manager. "Development" is essentially fund-raising, and every non-state-supported ballet company in the world needs a regular infusion of money. No company can operate successfully if it depends solely on box office receipts; other, greater sources must be tapped. This is the job of the development people. They seek additional funds for the company, whether through grants, performance fees, donations, or special promotions. They "develop" the company's financial structure and look to keep it solvent.

You will not meet these people often; sometimes they do not even work in the same building as you do. But you should know what they do because occasionally their work can create problems for your work. Lisa, a member of the Princeton Ballet, offers an example: "We were asked to dance at a gala recently, and the guests had cocktails and dinner first; then we came on. We didn't want to eat a big meal before we danced, but by the time we did eat the food was cold. We never got a chance to socialize with the audience because they left right after the performance. We went to development the next day and suggested that next year we dance *before* the meal. They were delighted we cared; they hadn't realized that it made such a difference to us."

Treat the development people as you do other nonartistic staff: be friendly, encouraging, sympathetic. Their role in the company may not seem as dramatically urgent as yours, for example, but without their sure hand in finding funding, whatever drama you might seek within the company may only come as the company closes its doors forever.

Remember . . . *dancers do not live by dance alone!*

In the Theatre   4

*The dancer's first job is to get into the light, to dance in
the spot. They can do the best dancing in the world, but
if they aren't in the light, they aren't going to be seen.*
—Taffy Waters, former production manager,
Brooklyn Academy of Music

Taffy Waters has worked in the theatre for thirty years, always behind the curtain but responsible for shows and ballet perform- ances on both sides of the Atlantic. If the stage is the dancer's kingdom, then backstage is *his* realm, and he leaves the definite impression that a young dancer should be aware of that. And backstage is indeed a realm, more than a location.

Waters maintains that backstage is not simply a cave to shield the dancer from an encroaching public; nor is it a playground or relaxation center. Things happen backstage, important things, crucial things, and what goes on there is as much a part of the dancer's art as the ribbons on her shoes.

"I think if a dancer could remember that even if they are the ones whose names are in the program, even if they are the ones who are in the spotlight, their performance depends to a great extent on a lot of other people in the background," he says, the years of experience weighing on his words. "It's a bit humbling, I suppose, but there's almost no point in dancers dancing their hearts out on stage if they can't be seen; there's no point in dancing their hearts out if all of a sudden their jacket flies off or they lose a shoe or if a piece of scenery falls down and takes the audience's attention away."

A performance really has to be a coming together of the efforts and the will of so many people, and dancers should consider themselves lucky indeed that they are the ones out on stage receiving accolades while the people backstage toil in relative obscurity to make it possible. But don't make the mistake of wrapping your arms around those accolades and cradling them as your own because Taffy Waters will tell you that he and his people deserve as many as you do. This is not a solo magic show.

When asked what is the most important thing a young dancer should learn from him, he chuckles, but his words have force. "Keep out of the bloody way backstage!"

You arrive at the theatre, move quickly to your dressing room, and begin to get ready for rehearsal. You share the dressing room with three other girls, corps members all, and you suddenly remember your teacher's words from years before: "The way you behave backstage is a mirror of the way you will dance on stage. Ballet is like a huge iceberg," she had explained quietly, "what the audience sees is what the mariner sees—the tip only. But there is more, much more beneath the surface, and that is what allows the tip to be seen."

You shake your head at the mess of clothes and remnants your dressing room mates have dropped casually about, nothing hung up, nothing laid out unwrinkled. You are horrified because you know that the way your ballet working clothes are dealt with is the way you ultimately feel about your art. Sloppy personal habits, sloppy dancing . . . no discipline in the dressing room, no discipline on stage.

You unpack your bag, noting you've arrived well before your dressing room mates and happy for the privacy. A small space alive with four energetic young bodies can be stifling. You also know that your early arrival will give you added time to prepare for the upcoming rehearsal, and you won't feel the pressure of a quick warm-up and an uncertain first few moves. You smooth a towel on the table and methodically line up your stage makeup, base brushes, shadows, q-tips, pencils, rouges, mascara, and lipsticks. To the side you place cream remover for after the performance, hairbrush, combs, hairpins, bobby pins, elastic hair bands and nets, spray, gel, and mousse. You giggle a bit, thinking how complicated it all can be, yet you know the audience cares only for the final product and *they* would notice if something wasn't where it should be.

Ah, you sigh, catching sight of your good-luck brown teddy bear peeking from behind the mirror. It was the one your teacher had given you when you got your first apprentice contract, and the bear has followed you since. Its soft dark eyes and wiggly ears offer some hope of wisdom, you think, or is it simply nostalgia?

"So many superstitions in the theatre," your teacher had explained, "no one should be without her own charm." She had talked about never putting

Each dancer's personal touch. © Patricia Brain.

Careful attention must be taken so not a single hair is out of place. Dianne Partington, Les Grands Ballets Canadiens. © Patricia Brain.

new ballet shoes on the table because it brought bad luck, about eating an M&M before each rehearsal or audition, about never whistling backstage.

You lay out a leotard and tights for yourself, then begin to apply your makeup. You feel confident, and you can sense your body tingling with anticipation. You're happy to be a dancer.

One of the odd things about backstage ballet is the relatively small role played by the stage manager. We know, for example, that this person "calls the show," that he or she acts as liaison between the production staff and the artistic staff. The stage manager sits in the "prompt corner" and is the first line of assistance should an emergency erupt on stage.

An important role, certainly.

But less important in ballet than other performing arts. Why? Here's Taffy Waters again: "Because there is the ballet master between the stage manager and the dancers. In any other form of theatre the stage manager is next in line to the director and takes over rehearsals in the absence of the director. But in ballet the ballet master is much more responsible for discipline and the ballet master takes rehearsals."

Dancers, in effect, have little contact directly with the stage manager, but you must be aware of one thing, be on the lookout for it, and guide yourself accordingly. "It's essential," emphasizes Taffy Waters, "that there be a very close working relationship between the ballet master and the stage manager; if they are at odds, they will be constantly undermining one another."

And guess who suffers then?

What sort of thing might come between a ballet master and stage manager? Taffy Waters remembers one circumstance: "Once we had a ballet master who used to kick the curtain in order to get another curtain call, and it would really annoy me. Say you'd already had three curtain calls, if there was the hope of getting another one, this ballet master would run forward and kick the curtain as if there was action going on backstage, and this would give the audience the sense of 'oh, they're still there!' So they'd give another call. It probably has a root in vaudeville, but this type of thing has no place in ballet."

Under these circumstances a disapproving stage manager could be a formidable foe since he or she controls the curtain. Without realizing it dancers could find themselves in the middle, subject to embarrassment, even downright humiliation, if it came to that.

So, read that relationship between ballet master and stage manager and decide how it will affect you.

Things are a bit different in Europe and Great Britain, if only because the stage manager is more highly regarded than in the United States. The stage manager is part of the artistic-creative force in the company, taking over any time the director is unavailable. (In the United States such a responsibility would be performed by the ballet master.) The stage manager handles such things as auditions and rehearsals, and no one would think to question his interpretation of style or ballet expression. Taffy Waters sums it up in one pithy phrase: "In Great Britain the stage manager is regarded as GOD!"

You sit back, makeup on, leotard, tights, and skirt fitted. Your eye touches the lovely white silk you wore at the last performance in the vision scene of *Sleeping Beauty,* and you remember the stifling space limits and struggling bodies as the four of you had to change simultaneously for every act that evening. Four of you in one dressing room, sharing one union dresser, hearing the stage manager's five-minute-interval calls to curtain and wondering if you'd make it.

The white silk hung so gracefully, so delicately; it belied the frenzy of the four of you that evening.

You giggle as you remember one of the girls trying to speed things along and reaching for her costume before the union dresser was ready for her.

"Better not do that, sweetie," the middle-aged dresser had said, still fussing over another girl. You remember thinking the dresser resembled your gym teacher back in high school. Sturdy, square, large red hands.

"Union rules, remember?"

The girl had flushed and nodded. Of course you all knew that since this was a union house, union dressers were required when you stepped into a costume and fastened it. You couldn't even pick up the costume without a union dresser.

Sometimes, though, you'd forget, especially when the stage manager was making everyone nervous with his five-minute-interval calls.

Of course he's just doing his job, you know all about that, but still . . .

You sigh, thinking how soft the silk felt that evening, how thoroughly regal! A good union dresser would prepare the costume this way, and you were grateful for that. Grateful, too, now that you thought of it, that dressers are part of the ballet world—from delivering and repairing costumes, to helping with costume changes and keeping track of pointe shoes, to packing up costumes again and readying them for the next performance.

You offer a final lingering look at your newly ironed and cleaned silk and push yourself to your feet. You know it's time to warm up before rehearsal.

One of the more confusing things about backstage life in a ballet company is that there could be two different people, each with the title "manager," each responsible for company performances, each necessary if dancers are to appear on stage in front of an audience.

The stage manager and the company manager. The stage manager, remember, operates his fief *on stage,* in the prompt corner, "calling the show," running the stage hands, and sitting with the artistic director during rehearsals. The company manager operates his fief away from the stage, planning the company's travel, counting box office receipts, writing out checks, doing payroll, balancing the books, and contending with the steady flush of paperwork.

If the stage manager's realm is the stage, then the company manager's realm is the office and the box office. Here is Taffy Waters on the difference between the two jobs: "The company manager is responsible for the bus and all the musicians and dancers, while the stage manager is responsible for the truck and the stage crew and the loading of props and costumes. The company manager should stay with the company [meaning the dancers], and the stage manager should stay with the stage personnel."

He reflects for a moment: "When I was stage manager with the Pennsylvania Ballet and we were on tour, the company manager would travel with the company. They left the hotel at nine in the morning, went by bus, and arrived at the theatre by about four in the afternoon. But I had already left the night before, traveled straight through, and arrived at the theatre at eight that morning and began to put the show out—before the company had even started by bus!"

An obvious question needs to be asked: Could both jobs—stage manager and company manager—be done by the same person?

Taffy Waters' answer is emphatic: "Not if both jobs are being done correctly. If a company tries to double up the jobs, one side will suffer. The checks will be late, or the company is going to feel neglected, or there will be a truck that's lost and no one will know it until four in the afternoon because the stage manager had been acting as company manager for a few hours. It never works."

You walk on stage and find a quiet corner, slowly warming up your feet, legs, back, neck, and arms. Then you put on pointe shoes, seeking to work on special steps you need for the demi-soloist role you've been asked to understudy. Few of the company have arrived so early, and you recall your teacher's insistence upon a continuing professional attitude no matter how far one had progressed with a ballet career: "Dedication, it's what separates the gifted amateur from the professional. You must do your work six days a week, each week throughout the season; you must check your costume each time you put it on; you must check your cues before each performance; you must dedicate yourself to doing the best job you can in the role that you are in—whether it's corps or soloist—each day, every day. It is not enough to rely upon some magic formula to get you through. You are a professional. You must act like one!"

Dancers must doublecheck that nothing is hanging loose from their pointe shoes. Dianne Partington, Les Grands Ballets Canadiens. © Patricia Brain.

Such as coming to rehearsal early, such as dedicating yourself to complete command of your ballet roles, you realize.

Your eyes drop to your toes, to your pointe shoes, and you see a trailing ribbon . . . how could that have happened? Quickly, you crouch to retie it . . . and you remember that sad story about Mary, with whom you apprenticed—was it only three years ago? Poor Mary, she had been so

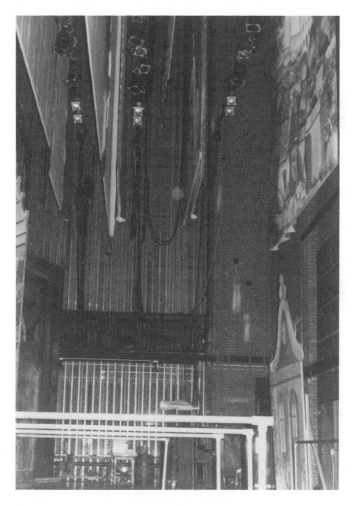

A view of the stage with warmup barres and scenery, and overhead are hanging lights and a backdrop stored in the fly space. © James Whitehill.

excited when the artistic director had offered her a demi-soloist role—you were envious, you remembered—and she had worked so hard on it. She was such a careful dancer, too, but she had been having trouble with her Achilles tendon, so the wardrobe mistress had sewn an insert of elastic into the ribbon which Mary herself had sewn onto her pointe shoe, trying to soften the stiffness. Poor Mary, she had taken her first sauté arabesque onto the stage, and the ribbon popped; the audience gasped, but Mary danced on, never missing a beat, even though inside she felt the horrors of total embarrassment and uncertainty. She knew, and she knew her partner knew, that both of them were in danger. Somehow Mary got through the ballet, but three months later when contract talks came up, Mary was not taken into the company, even though no one could really blame her for what happened.

You notice some technical work is going on around you. Electricians are working on lights hanging from a long pipe that had been lowered to the stage. They are adding square metal frames with different-colored transparencies—called gels—in order to be able to change stage lighting moods, depending upon the ballet to be performed.

"Try the reds and blues," you hear over a loudspeaker, and you know it's the lighting director in his booth high over the audience trying out different combinations with the electricians.

You realize, of course, that it's not only the dancers who are rehearsing. For everyone in the company, backstage life is a recurrent cycle of create, plan, rehearse, and perform. Everyone is involved.

You push yourself high on pointe, holding it far longer than you'll need for any current performance. You recall your teacher's prophetic words: "Backstage life is the heartbeat of a ballet company. What happens there will tell us if the company lives or dies."

You look around; you sense excitement. You see other corps members taking their places at the barre. You see the ballet master walking briskly on stage from the wings. You release your pointe, and you feel good.

This company is alive, warm-up class is about to begin, and you are important.

Outside the Theatre   5

Whether shopping, eating out, or attending official
receptions, dancers must be "on"!
                    —*Eddy Toussaint, artistic director,*
                                    Ballet de Montréal

*D*ance is a way of life. How you carry yourself, how you face the world proclaims: "I AM A DANCER!" As a professional you are always "on" because you are your instrument, even when injured or on tour, whether visiting the doctor or disembarking from a six-hour flight.

Unlike the nine-to-five worker or the piecework technician, you do not leave your job at the office; you do not stop being a dancer merely because you have walked out of the stage door. A dancer's art is in her being. It projects from her wherever she is: on stage, in daily class, at the supermarket, in a restaurant, on the sidewalk.

Margot Fonteyn, prima ballerina assoluta, wrote in her 1972 autobiography: "The audience is always right. They buy their tickets in expectation of entertainment, laughter, beauty, tears, intellectual exercise or whatever. If they are disappointed, it is our fault, not theirs. Every performance carries a burden of responsibility, and the performer must strive to match the expectations of the public."

The performance burden carries over to the dancer's life outside the theatre. Imagine how jarring it would be for a ballet patron who had seen you perform *Giselle* the night before to come upon you the next day at the supermarket checkout line and you appear with scraggly hair, tattered clothes, and a disagreeable frown. Imagine how easy it would be for this ballet patron to pass the word that "she certainly looks different when she's out of costume!"

Imagine how quickly the magic of your performance could fly away as ballet patrons think what you could be *really* like!

For many dancers the most difficult test is maintaining their professional attitude when they are not dancing. It's hard to be out of work, it's especially hard to be injured, but these are the times when it's important to remember that dance is a way of life. A dancer has responsibilities not only to herself but to her profession and to the very nature of her art form. You remain a dancer, and all that it means, whether you are working inside the theatre or existing outside of it. In the words of one well-known artistic director, "We are not gypsies; we are ambassadors of dance." It's in your best interests to keep that in mind.

ON TOUR

> *It was only later when we covered 102 towns in six or seven months that it [touring] stopped being an art and started being what in Russia we call a "gig."*
> —*Alexandra Danilova, prima ballerina assoluta of Ballet Russe de Monte Carlo*

"*We're going on tour!*" The word has filtered from artistic director to ballet master to principals and finally to corps de ballet. Touring . . . that exciting, adventurous step that has bred a thousand tales for young dancers to exchange. "When I was on tour in Australia . . . "; "One night while I was on tour in Sweden . . . "; "If you ever tour Brazil, well, . . . !"

"*We're going on tour!*" The words echo again and again as you read over the itinerary and the instruction sheets, remembering the comments of the artistic director: "We do a biennial tour of Europe, and this year we plan to begin in Italy. We'll be gone about three months."

The questions fly through your mind: What do I pack? Is my present passport current? Do they speak English? How will I get around? . . .

The basic thing to understand about touring is that it's all part of your contract. The section referring to travel covers your transportation, meal allowances, and a regular per diem rate.

The first tour, of course, is full of uncertainties, especially if you've never traveled far from home. Almost every major ballet company tours, not always to Europe but somewhere. And a tour means exactly that—a touchdown at a series of places, with performances each day or evening (sometimes twice a day) usually a long distance from home. Of course if the tour is to Europe or some other well-developed part of the world, you won't need to stock up on cosmetics, toiletries, drugs, and other incidentals of civilization. These things are present in abundance where you will be dancing. Obviously, though, if you will be touring in an underdeveloped part of the world, you should seek guidance from other dancers who may have already performed there, as well as from your company manager, since he or she has access to whatever information you need. If neither of these choices is appropriate, then use your head and plan to take what you need. But be careful. Space, you will find, is limited. You have to provide for yourself for a period of weeks, perhaps months, and you can't lug a steamer trunk or two with you on tour. (At times you may have to carry your own luggage.) Take what you need, but *only* what you need. Nothing more.

All of this leads to packing, which, as you probably know, is a concern for any theatre person, even if it's just a weekend away. What gets packed and how it gets packed are crucial when you consider that a company on tour must arrange to transport every dancer's personal baggage, *in addition* to costumes, sets, and lights. The logistics can be staggering.

Packing. A wise father, one day, spoke to his young dancer-daughter as she was preparing to go on her first tour. "Pack your bag with everything you want to take," he said. "Carry it out to the car, then turn around and carry it back inside. Take half the contents out and return the bags to the car."

"But, Dad, I'll have so much room."

"Think of how much space you'll have to bring home new things," he said.

If you are touring internationally, you will need a passport, and these take time to get, especially if you've never had one. You'll need a certified copy of your birth certificate ("certified" means that the clerk of the office that handles these things in your city of birth—Bureau of Vital Statistics, for instance—must stamp and sign the certificate copy; a simple xerox copy won't do), two passport photos, one additional form of identification (such as a driver's license, Social Security card), and processing fees. The first place to start should be your county clerk's office.

When you're on tour, you will usually have a tour guide and interpreter to help with the language and familiarize you with customs. Pay careful attention to what they say, and don't assume you can disregard their instructions.

Young dancers sometimes do forget. Mary Day, artistic director of the Washington Ballet, tells of this incident from a South American tour: "We went up on a funicular to the top of a mountain. We were told not to walk down, and most of the dancers obeyed and rode the funicular back down. But three of the dancers thought, 'There are crowds of people walking so let's walk too,' and before they got to the bottom their purses were stolen."

You never know what awaits you as you get off the bus in a new town—it may even be a friend. Dianne Partington, Les Grands Ballets Canadiens. © James Whitehill.

Touring *is* traveling, sometimes by bus through the night. You will need to develop a set of exercises to stretch out the kinks, similar to those you do before class but with more emphasis on stretching. Sometimes you must go directly from the bus into class—a new city, a new performance to ready.

Organization makes a difference. Pack a small overnight bag for long bus tours. Include a good book, stationery to write to friends and family, an inflatable pillow and lightweight blanket (the kind they have on planes), maps and brochures of the countryside you will pass, light snacks and juice, and magnetic travel games such as backgammon or a pack of cards. A board game such as Trivial Pursuit can keep you entertained for days and days.

Touring will always have a special allure. What is there about it that excites a young dancer and keeps that adventurous glow from month to month, year to year? Here's what Rochelle Zide Booth says: "I just love the traveling and going to different places and different cities. Also it's a fact that this is a time when the company really feels like a family. You come to rely so much on one another because you are a stranger wherever you go, and that isn't the case, of course, when you're in your city of residence." At home young dancers have a life outside the company. You leave rehearsal and slide back into the personal life you have created for yourself; what transpires at the company is simply an eight-hour aberration in a much longer day. It isn't an encompassing life by any means; it is just a segment of your day.

But on tour much of that feeling disappears. "In a touring company people learn to make friends within the company," Rochelle Zide Booth continues, "to see each other whether or not they are on tour, and that carries over even when they return home. You'll find much more often that people who are in touring companies leave rehearsals together, go off to the movies, to the museum, to the library together. In nontouring companies they will leave rehearsals singly and slip back into their other world. It's a pity because dancers in nontouring companies are just not as committed to their companies."

Once you arrive at your destination you are assigned to your room (usually in a hotel, usually near the theatre). The stage or company manager issues your per diem and gives you directions to the theatre and information about restaurants open after the performance. If there is a reception planned, he tells you where it will be held and whether you can expect to be fed or not. You may also be given information about local points of interest.

Certainly there are exciting things to see and do on tour. Richard Englund, artistic director of Joffrey II, remembers the time he and the company were performing in Fargo, North Dakota. He discovered that the Gage family, which is also his wife's family, was prominent and respected. There was a Gage Museum and a Gage artistic collection. "I learned so much," he says. "That's where Frank Baum, who wrote *The Wizard of Oz,* lived. And all the history of the book came to life! The town had facades with Arabic motifs and pillars and a women's drill team which had inspired the Emerald City drill team in the movie. Some of the drawings in the book are based on buildings in the city. It was just incredible!"

You continue to receive your paycheck while you're on tour, and the pay dates will be the same schedule you're familiar with. The company manager (or stage manager) can tell you at which local bank they have made arrangements for you to cash your check. Many dancers find that per diem is enough and either don't cash their checks (which is not smart because checks can be lost or stolen, and some banks may refuse to cash them if they are two or three months old) or have the company make direct deposits into their accounts (which is smarter).

Touring can be a time to save. Apprentices choose to share their rooms with three or four other dancers, thus saving on hotel fees, although some companies issue per diem only for food, and the company pays the hotel bills.

There is a type of attitude which takes to touring, a sort of special personality which finds constant packing and unpacking, different beds almost every night, unfamiliar foods, and uncertain customs an adventure. It's a blend of curiosity, self-confidence, and simple challenge: Will I

Wardrobe cases carry dancers' make-up and shoes. These travel with the sets and costumes.
© James Whitehill.

survive this, and if I do, what kind of person will I become? What can I learn, what can I carry with me for the rest of my life from this experience?

Rochelle Zide Booth tells this story of the simple way Ballet Russe de Monte Carlo separated those with a touring inclination from those without one: "They used to say that if you came back for the second year, you would stay at least five years, and if you came back after five years, you would stay for life. We did lose a lot of people after one year." The company would leave New York the first of October and return the middle of May. (That's a seven-month tour!) Then, after a short break, there would be a summer tour as well. "That's a long time to be away from home," she adds, and most would agree.

On the other side, touring can be such a boon to a young dancer with that special attitude, that urge for travel. Robert Englund tells of the time he and Joffrey II were in Greece: "There was a wonderful museum and some nearby excavations not far from Athens. Everything was closed when we were there, but we got them to open it so the kids could go and see the gold collections and the things from the tombs. Some of those dancers will never be quite the same because of that opportunity." He considers this type of exposure an educational opportunity, a concept which sometimes escapes parents who tend to concentrate on the more traditional benefits of formal schooling. "Education is important," he insists, "but there is the kind of an education that a dancer gets or can get that is so rare and so unique and unusual that it opens up a mind and lets them have the kind of experience they would never have at an isolated school."

Of course, the benefits of touring must always be weighed against the demands of your schedule. If the company is performing for a lengthy period in one location or within a narrow geographic radius, life tends to be more settled, and you won't have to pack up and rush . . . travel and unpack . . . rehearse on a strange stage in a strange theatre, sleep in a strange bed . . . and then start the process over the next day. But sometimes, your tour is of the one-night-stand variety, and then touring is more of an endurance affair than anything else! You don't get to see much of the area in which you're performing—except for the theatre where you dance and the hotel where you eat and sleep—because you are on the road again and again and again.

Rochelle Zide Booth tells an amusing story about one-night-stand touring. "Sometimes you never really know where you are. I remember one time somebody came up to me at a party and asked, 'Where are you going tomorrow?' I had memorized the tour, I knew the order of the itinerary, and I had to say, 'Where am I today?' And when she told me, I could tell her where I was going tomorrow, and where I had been yesterday. But without her help I just didn't know."

The discipline you have learned over the years must now be applied outside the studio. Schedule your time so that you get a good night's sleep when you are staying in hotels. Arrange for wake-up calls early enough so that you can see the local highlights. Know how far away the theatre is and how long it will take you to get there. Learn the local customs and be careful not to get lost while exploring.

Heed this story of two dancers—neither of whom was a U.S. citizen—who should have known better. They were performing in the United States, not far from the Mexican border, when they decided to walk across. Unfortunately they didn't bother taking their passports. When they tried to return, they found they had to go through immigration, and since they didn't have their passports, they were detained until they could be vouched for by their companies and counsels. One of the dancers missed her performance that evening. Her understudy went on and performed so well she retained the part for the rest of the tour.

There certainly are differences between touring in Europe and touring in the United States. The most obvious is the language situation—natives of Italy, France, Germany, and other countries might know English, but it is not their primary language. Most of them *think* in their primary language, even if they speak English, and you should be respectful of and try to understand their culture. For example, recently Ballet de Montréal was performing in Pompeii, Italy, and warm-up was held in one of the excavated sites. A young dancer used a wall for balance and, while doing a grand battement, loosened a brick, and some mortar settled to the floor. Instead of proceeding, the ballet master stopped class and summoned the archaeological maintenance staff who carefully replaced the brick and steadied the wall, after mentioning that the site was a particularly fine example of old Roman architecture. A month later when the company returned to its home studio, the Marley floor was rolled out . . . and there! in a little pile was some of the Pompeian dust, a memento to the careful respect shown another way of life.

"You are coping with a different culture," says ballet master David Howard about touring in Europe (or anywhere else in the world for that matter). "You are put into 'pensions' instead of motels or hotels sometimes; you are in different kinds of theatres. You know every country has a different smell, and you are aware of it as soon as you arrive at the airport. No matter whether you go to Italy, France, Switzerland, Germany, each country has its smell, and you are aware of it as you get there." Howard refers to this smell as an "aroma," special to the country, special to you. "I always find when I go to Europe that even the guy who drives the local tram knows what is going on at the Opera House; they are aware, much more than in the United States.

"In Europe, ballet is a strong part of the cultural scene. It is appreciated in a way that does not seem to exist in the United States," Howard continues. Some may disagree with him, but the point is that ballet companies in Europe perform on the finest stages, in the most elegant theatres, and before the most knowledgeable audiences. Wouldn't any American dancer going on a European tour find this breathtaking?

But whether you tour Europe, the United States, or any other country, enjoy the experience, pace yourself, and learn as much as possible. Remember you are an emissary for your company, your art, and in some instances your country.

Bon voyage!

Touring can take you to exotic places. Les Grands Ballet Canadiens at Kyoto City. © Deirdre Kelly.

INJURY

*The worst thing a dancer can do is try to jump back in
as if nothing has happened.*
                    —Rochelle Zide Booth, *master teacher*

Scratch a dancer, probe the private core, reach waaaaaaay inside,
the innermost part . . . face the monster, stare its eye down, ask the question . . .

"What's a dancer's worst nightmare?"

A chorus responds . . . *"Injury!"*

Not . . . "I'm afraid of falling off the stage . . . I fear forgetting my
choreography . . . I'm scared of unemployment."

Injury! The biggest fear.

For good reason too. As technique has accelerated, choreography has
made substantially more and different demands on the body, and as
dancers come into companies at younger and younger ages, the rash of
injuries grows in proportion to the growing pains inflicted on these young
bodies. Physical immaturity, while masked by flowing technique for a
while, can bring about career-threatening injury that would not be so
severe in a more physically mature dancer.

Even so, some aspects of medical treatment for injuries have kept pace
with these changing demands. Ten years ago, for example, a dancer with a
severely ripped ligament could expect to see her career shortened
substantially. She might be offered minor roles for a few years, but certainly
nothing major. Now, however, surgery for this same injury uses
transplants, synthetics, or the body's own fascia, and the ripped ligament
does not become the albatross it once was. The scars from the surgery are
barely noticeable (compare *that* with ten years ago!), the recovery periods
are shorter, and physical therapy is less grueling and produces better
results. Dancers are returning to the work force for longer careers, often
stronger than before.

What are *my* chances of injury, you might ask? Pretty substantial, is the
answer. According to *Dance Magazine,* in a 1982–83 study of professional
and advanced dancers conducted by Ballet West, ninety percent (that's nine
out of ten!) of the professional dancers and sixty-three percent of the
advanced students had been injured severely enough at some point in their
careers to affect their dancing.

If you were going to play Russian roulette, and added a second bullet to one of the chambers, your chances would still be better than these figures show. Can you expect that you'll be injured severely enough to stop dancing—at least temporarily—at some point in your career?

Yes! A resounding yes, the answer seems to be.

First then, you must understand what you can do to *prevent* such an injury. Prevention is the best and surest way to ward the monster off, and there are certain things you can do:

- *A good diet.* Food is the fuel of energy and strength, and even though you may feel you have to stay thin, there's a tiny line between thin and *too* thin. Heed the words of one artistic director: "anexoria and bulimia are injuries, too," and avoid the candy bar quick fix or fast food fill-up.

- *Sleep.* The performance ends at 10:30, it takes a half hour to get dressed and out of the theatre, and you're starving. An hour and a half for dinner, and it's past midnight before you get home. Then you need to wash out your tights and unwind. Class is at 9:30 the next morning, and you see it's after two before you turn off the light . . . Oh well, you think, I'll take a nap after class. *How many times do you take a nap?*

- *Be fully warmed up before class.* Fifteen to twenty minutes before class could save months of misery because your muscles weren't stretched properly.

- *Know what your body needs.* Don't slack off during layoff periods. Create a personal system to keep limber and supple so you are ready to start work each season.

- *Pace yourself.* Beware of fatigue; cut back when you're feeling overwhelmed. LISTEN TO YOUR BODY!

But suppose you do get injured, what then? The first thing a young dancer frets over is his or her performance responsibility. "I can't let this happen," you say, "someone else will get my part!"

Not necessarily. Rochelle Zide Booth, formerly with the Joffrey Ballet and now a renowned master teacher, offers an approach that many artistic directors follow: "If it appears to be a minor sprain, even if there is some swelling, then I will say, 'We are going to ice it first, and then there are two choices: You're in rehearsal, there's no performance for a couple weeks, so get off it and get it well'; OR 'We're in performance, you are going to get off this leg, but you don't have to get off it now. You can ice it, take some aspirin; you may perform if you want to. But immediately, IMMEDIATELY, after the performances are over, you must have it taken care of.' "

A careful warm up is imperative to avoid injury. Always be conscious of your placement. Left: Anik Bissonette, Les Grands Ballets Canadiens. © Patricia Brain. Right: Dianne Partington, Les Grands Ballets Canadiens. © Patricia Brain.

A major problem for any injured dancer is a sense of identity loss: "If I can't dance, what can I do? . . . Dancing is my life . . . it's what I'm trained to do."

Alan Goldberg, a sports psychologist who has been treating dancers for years, doesn't see injury as the disaster many young dancers assume it is even if the injury is career-ending. "What dancers fail to realize," he says, "is that in the process of learning to be a dancer, they've disciplined themselves, they've learned incredibly important skills. It merely becomes a question of helping them with the loss and the depression and the anger and all of the stages of grief until they're ready to take the strategies they used to become successful as a dancer and reapply them in other arenas of life. It's a question of working on self-esteem and applying those strategies to be successful in other areas."

That's when the injury is career-ending. But what if the injury is *not* career-ending?

Then another mind-set is appropriate. Two key words—*Patience!* . . . *Determination!*

Be patient, be determined. You will recover, you will go on, you won't rush, you won't itch.

- "See ten movies you've always wanted to see," suggests Rochelle Zide Booth.
- "Learn something new," offers Richard Englund of Joffrey II.
- "I left dance completely when I broke my foot," says Teresina, a former member of the Tulsa Ballet.
- "I drove a cab," says Frank, a company member with the Ballet Iowa.
- "I think dancers who are injured and then sit around and watch tend to go down deeper and get more neurotic," says Becky, formerly with the Dayton Ballet. "Immediately after I got my cast off, I went into therapy and started working. You spend so much time in the studio, so much time rehearsing, I think you miss out on other things that are going on around the world."

Knowing that you love to dance can bolster your attitude as well as deflate it. If you're injured, it's much easier to feel sorry for yourself than to revel in the fact that dance has been and always will be the single most joyful thing you have ever done. See what these young dancers—all having suffered severe injury—say about that!

- "I sat around and got fat, and I felt sorry for myself, until one day I looked in the mirror and asked myself what I wanted out of life. I realized that what I wanted was to dance because it made me happy. There are too many people in the world doing things they don't enjoy."
- "I found that there was nothing else I loved to do."
- "I learned that a job is a job, and whatever I was doing I had to give it my all. I realized that dance is no different from any other job, just that this is what I enjoy doing the most."

But the injury equation is two-sided: You should know how to handle yourself when you are not dancing; you should not allow yourself to curl into a ball of sorrow and sadness and sloppiness. You should think positively, and you should act the same way. The other side of the equation, however, is just as important and just as tricky: You should be able to seek out the "right" medical care to treat your injury.

The *right* medical care! Not all medical care is equal—most seasoned dancers will tell you this. Simply because a friendly, sympathetic, earnest medical professional has "Dr." in front of his or her name doesn't mean that physician can—or should—diagnose and treat your injury. This is especially true if your injury is serious and requires surgery or a cast. For those of you who live and work in major urban centers, there are usually enough highly specialized sports medicine physicians to go around, and most major dance studios have a ready list.

For those in less populated areas, though, the problem is clear: the number of specialists and the work they do are functions of the population they serve. The smaller the population, the less opportunity for a physician to specialize and the less sophisticated the treatment available. This equation can even affect dancers in a major center like New York City. Rochelle Zide Booth explains: "The big problem that dancers have now is that if they are not in the New York City Ballet, American Ballet Theatre, or Joffrey companies they can't even get to see the good doctors." What she means is that experienced sports medicine physicians are spoken for weeks and months in advance, and their availability is often scooped up by dancers and companies whose reputations demand priority attention. "Heaven help you," Rochelle Zide Booth adds, "if you are in a smaller company."

And she means a smaller company in New York City, too.

Yet things don't have to be that bleak, no matter where you may be dancing. Suppose you're injured, and you aren't near a major urban center. You've been given the name of a doctor, someone you know nothing about. The first and most important thing you do is ask questions! The answers will determine whether you should move on.

Ask:

• *Have you ever worked on a dancer?* (Some doctors consider it a violation of doctor-patient confidentiality to divulge names, but you should insist on an answer to whether this doctor has faced dancers' injuries.)

• *Have you treated this type of injury before?*

• *Have you performed your recommended procedure successfully with others?*

• *What will be my recovery period?*

• *How much physical therapy will be required?*

• *Where will the physical therapy take place?*

• *Are there facilities close at hand?*

You should expect responsive and satisfying answers to each of these questions. If not, move on.

Remember, not all sports medicine people are equal; not all understand the special needs of young dancers. Think of this story about Collette, still only twenty-two but a veteran of three companies in four years. At this moment her career hangs by a tiny thread, but two years ago she had nothing but a dazzling future to excite her days. True, she did have an aching knee, and so one day she went to see a therapist in Montreal where her company was performing. He prescribed exercises and a few days' rest, and sure enough, the knee began to feel better. She went back to work and finished out the season without further problem.

A year later she was doing soloist work with a company in the Midwest, and as she took a preparation for a tour jeté, she felt a stab of pain in the same knee and fell heavily. This time it wasn't just an ache—she hurt. Someone suggested a local sports medicine physician, and Collette gathered herself together and limped to his office.

"A sprained ligament," he diagnosed. "Here are some crutches and stay off it for a while."

But a month later it was no better. She couldn't dance and the pain was severe. So she had intensive X-ray and radium therapy, and it showed there might be ligament damage.

"I doubt it," the doctor said, "let's give things another month."

No dancing, no dancing, and still the pain remained.

"Let's do an exploratory arthroscopy," the doctor offered after the second month. By this time Collette was happy to do *anything!*

What they found guaranteed to put Collette on the dance shelf for the next year: a ripped ligament that would have to be cut out and reconstruction performed—a procedure rightly described as major surgery because, if not done correctly, her career would be ended.

And it all started because she had a small ache in her knee.

Treating an injury properly implies that someone is going to have to pay for that treatment. It can get expensive. Look at Collette's visits to the doctors, her surgical experiences, and the rehabiliation she must now face. Expensive, expensive, and she won't be able to dance for at least a year.

The savior is workman's compensation, a form of insurance that ballet companies (all companies, in fact) must have to protect employees who are injured on the job. Remember that key phrase . . . *on the job.* If you are injured and it is not job related, you can't take advantage of workman's compensation and have your medical bills picked up or your dance earnings salvaged.

Workman's compensation is state mandated; that is in most states the law requires it just the same as it requires automobile liability insurance.

Workman's compensation is considered insurance because it *protects* you from something; it doesn't reward you for doing or not doing something. The premiums for workman's compensation insurance are paid by your employer, and you are the one who benefits . . . should you be injured.

How much money might you expect to receive? Obviously, the answer depends to some extent on the nature of your injury, but the results can be surprising. "It gave me more benefits than I expected," says Rochelle Zide Booth, talking of the compensation she received while laid off due to a torn Achilles tendon she suffered some years ago. "It's hard for them to determine exactly how much, sometimes, because they have to decide how disabled you are, how much of a disability you have."

For example, if you operate a sewing machine, you could suffer the same leg injury as a dancer, but your sewing machine career wouldn't be in danger. The dancer, on the other hand, might never be able to dance again. So the insurer figures out how much of a disability each person suffered—usually a percentage of total disability (sixty percent disabled, forty-five percent disabled . . .)—and then fixes the award. So long as the injury is work related, the insurance company is obligated to pay all medical fees: doctor's visits, ambulances, hospital costs, surgery, rehabilitation, medical equipment and supplies, even prostheses, and, unlike personal health insurance, there is no deductible or ceiling on the amount paid.

Whatever it costs to get you whole, workman's compensation will pay.

But that's not all. Workman's compensation also pays a percentage of the salary you lose while you are recovering from your injury. Usually it pays about two-thirds of your take-home salary, subject to a maximum and minimum benefit set by your state, so at least you won't have to struggle with your injury *and* find a job to carry you from day to day. After you've been injured and are unable to work for three consecutive days, workman's compensation begins to cover your lost salary starting from day four. If you are still disabled by day ten, then workman's compensation picks up those first three days, so you won't lose a day of coverage.

And the reassuring thing is this: once you've returned to work, the workman's compensation clock begins ticking all over again. Three, five, or even ten years later, if you reinjure yourself *on the job* (work related, that is), your benefits (missed salary included) will resume. Workman's compensation protects you from having to face all those costs and expenses alone.

Now, let's suppose you have been injured, and you are facing therapy. Is it enough to rely on the average physical therapist in a hospital or office setting? Here's what Rochelle Zide Booth, after a lifetime of dancing and working with dancers, has to say: "Physical therapists think, sometimes, that if they can get you to walk down the street without turning your ankle, they have done their job. They know how to get rid of adhesions; they know how to get you started properly."

But, "they don't know a particular dancer's body. We, the intelligent dancers, know our bodies better than anyone else." What she means is that the problem with most physical therapy departments in hospitals or in offices is actually the same old story. No one there understands the demands of dance and dancers; no one there really understands how much further a dancer must go to attain rehabilitation and recovery. What suits a nondancer does not, certainly, suit a dancer.

"Awhile ago I had some problems with my knee, the first time that happened," Rochelle Zide Booth goes on. "Lord knows what was wrong with it, but I went to a doctor, and even before he examined me he said, 'Oh, you're a ballet dancer, I know what your problem is, you turn out too much from the knee down.' I said, 'I beg your pardon, I'm a teacher and I don't do that.' He answered: 'Oh yes, all ballet dancers do that.' I said, 'How do you make this judgment?' and he answered, 'I treat the Eglevsky Ballet; I'm right down the street from them.' I asked him to check my knee out, so he put me down on the table, and he said, 'I'll show you what I mean. Turn out from your hip.' Well, I happen to be very turned out from the hip, so my legs went flat out on the table. 'Oh dear,' he said, 'your problem is not turning out from your knee!' 'No,' I responded, 'dancers don't do that unless they've been badly trained.' "

The point is, this doctor made a generalization based on limited knowledge, and if his patient hadn't argued with him, he would have treated her for something that had nothing to do with her real injury. A waste of time, a waste of money, and possible disastrous consequences.

"That's not an isolated incident," Rochelle Zide Booth concludes. "It happens a lot."

Along with physical therapy comes emotional therapy—treatment of the mind as well as the body. An injury to one can often mean an injury to the other. "When a dancer is injured," says psychologist Alan Goldberg, "they feel as though they have lost their identity. It's the same with sports people: they've spent their whole lives doing this one thing; they think they know nothing else. If the injury is career threatening, it is devastating."

And this single-mindedness about a career has also developed a strong self-belief system—"I know I can dance," "I will succeed," "I will perform"—and the effect is to make it difficult to separate who you are from what you are. "I'm a dancer," you say, and that means so much more than having or doing a job. You live ballet, you breathe ballet, you don't just *do* ballet.

But the separation of who you are from what you are is necessary if you are going to understand yourself and cope adequately with injury. "Dancers' belief systems in themselves are so strong," Alan Goldberg continues, "that when the career is threatened, their whole being is threatened too." If I can't dance, what have I to live for? Dance is my life!

But Goldberg and other professionals offer help. "We try to help dancers explore themselves and find the person they really are. Once they learn that, then they can learn to separate the dancer from the person and start to build their self-confidence." Therapists work with performers, athletes, and gymnasts when they are mentally blocked by either injury or some aspect of their performance. "What happens," Alan Goldberg says, "is that your mind can fool your muscles. The brain sends messages through the nerves to the muscles, and the muscles start to move as they did when you were dancing. If the muscles are stimulated every day to remember what to do, by the time you are ready to start back, the muscles will be ready to start work again."

Injury, then, does not have to be an unending disaster. It may be a nightmare, but help is available, and you know others have gone through it. Remember, your body is your instrument. unlike a violinist, you can't go out and buy a new string and install it yourself. Your mind and your artistry, as with a musician, are the forces that make the instrument work. And like a musician, you must always listen to your instrument.

LAYOFF

> *When I'm on layoff, I take class at home, dance with*
> *small companies, go swimming, have a good vacation,*
> *but I still keep in good shape so that when I start up*
> *again, I'm ready.*
> —Timothy Miano, dancer, Dayton Ballet

Imagine a small company which offers a six- to eight-week contract in the late spring when most major companies are in a layoff period. Included are room, board, and a small salary. Imagine you are on layoff and wondering how to fill your time. Imagine talking of your dilemma with a former teacher, who responds: "I know where you might go . . ."

A telephone call, a short conversation, and you and that small company with its six- to eight-week contract have gotten together. You won't have to stop dancing during your layoff period. What you should know, however, is that your expectations must be refined to meet what this small company is able to provide.

Small companies, which satisfy many local dance needs, have limited budgets and often do not supply shoes and tights. Rehearsals may last two to three weeks, followed by three to four weeks of performance, combining lecture demonstrations—mostly in schools—and concerts throughout the state.

That is Vermont Ballet Theatre, and that is how dancers seeking to manage layoff time and a ballet company seeking dancers for a limited season have come together. One's need has become the other's solution. Repertoire is varied, touching on sections of the classics, pas de deux, and contemporary works, and all dancers are expected to dance the full repertoire. They come from other full-season companies throughout the United States and Canada, and they have the opportunity to dance major roles—which might be denied them in their present, full-season company—and to work and rehearse with accomplished choreographers and teachers.

Vermont Ballet Theatre is a haven for dancers on layoff. It is precisely because there is layoff time that Vermont Ballet Theatre was created. The company has its season during other companys' layoff times, and this makes it easy to hire dancers, develop a ballet program, and set up a performance schedule. No conflicts with other company contracts, no permanent resident-company expenses, no arduous struggle to fill out a thirty-five-week undertaking.

This, of course, is an unusual example because there aren't many ballet companies whose entire season begins and ends during a dancer's normal layoff time. But the point is this: opportunities grow out of need, and a dancer who will be on layoff should be alert to and plan for those circumstances which will give rise to these needs.

Layoff is a part of every dancer's life. Few ballet companies offer year-round contracts, so most young dancers face the reality that after a number of weeks of steady employment (the most usual number is thirty to forty) they will be laid off because the company's season has come to an end.

What to do, then, with this layoff period?

Damon, a young dancer with a midwestern ballet company, has a ready answer: "On layoff I always look for other work. I've been a waiter, taxi driver, tended bar, painted houses." He has to support himself, and he knows that whatever job he takes will have limited duration. It isn't as if he has to make a career-change decision. But he does know he wants to do something.

For the lucky few, layoff time doesn't exist. They are employed on a year-round basis, and they don't need to fill a succession of weeks each year with other gainful employment. New York City Ballet provides this, as does American Ballet Theatre and the San Francisco Ballet. No layoff time, no other-job worries.

In Europe the picture is a bit brighter. State-supported ballet companies such as England's Royal Ballet, Denmark's Royal Danish Ballet, Russia's Kirov and Bolshoi ballets, the Basel (Switzerland) Ballet, and the Paris Opéra Ballet are but a few of the foreign companies that employ their dancers full time and offer a complete career path. Dancers, in fact, often come to these companies in the blush of youth and remain with them throughout their ballet lives. As Terri, a young dancer with the Dayton Ballet, said while bemoaning her annual layoff employment search, "I like the contracts in Europe—contracts for life." It's not hard to understand her feelings. Wouldn't it be glorious to know that once you signed a company contract you needn't ever look for other ballet work, that your company will use you regularly throughout the year, that you have a place to dance year after year for as long as you wish it . . . providing your skills and technique keep pace?

Pity, then, the poor American dancer who must cope with layoff.

Or is it, perhaps, not as bad as it seems?

Layoff usually occurs in chunks of time—weeks at a stretch—and often that happens twice a year. The first occasion comes right after the rigors of *Nutcracker,* and for those dancers who have been performing daily throughout late November and most of December, it represents a well-deserved rest. Just a few weeks, really, time to visit friends or relatives, renew energy, and get ready for the resumption of an intense schedule, following shortly, that will focus on class, rehearsal, and performance.

The second—and longer—layoff period comes in mid to late spring and lasts until the summer shadows have begun to shorten, usually in August. You will have three to four months where company activities simply shut down, where you will have to support yourself, and where other dance opportunities are certainly limited. This is the layoff-time crunch, and a young dancer had better be prepared to cope with what could seem to be an endless stream of unmanaged days, waiting and waiting . . . until the company re-forms and rehearsals begin for the next season.

Once in a while a company structures itself and its performance schedule so young dancers have an easier time of it. Damon remembers well his first professional ballet job where he and the artistic director meshed neatly. Even the layoff-time crunch wasn't a problem. "I was employed eight to nine months but spread out through the year, so when I wasn't working, I was collecting unemployment." He enjoyed this split-season approach because it allowed him to feel he had only one employer and that he was a full-time employee. "It was really like a twelve-month job," he says, underscoring the uncertainty he might otherwise have felt if he had had to find extensive employment during a lengthy layoff period. "A lot of companies have twenty-seven to thirty-five week seasons, but these are all at one time, so the rest of the year you have to fend for yourself." He pauses, then shakes his head. "Usually, it's a struggle."

But not always. There are possibilities. Take dancing as a guest artist for regional or junior companies, for example. They have spring seasons, often extending weeks beyond the professional ballet company season, and they do have need for professional ballet assistance. What to do?

- Contact the nearest Dance America (formerly National Association of Regional Ballet Companies) office during your January layoff and get a list of close-by regional and junior companies.

- Write to the directors of those companies you would like to dance with, asking if they need a guest artist.

- Include a short résumé, but be sure to list your pas de deux and any principal roles you've danced or *that you know!*

- If they show interest, send a short video, *but* not more than ten minutes in length.

- Give them two or three weeks to respond, and if you haven't heard, get on the phone and find out why.

- Seek out available dance-oriented computerized information services (such as Dansource); provide them with your résumé and any other pertinent material.

- Above all, don't limit yourself to one company and one director. Spread yourself around, make multiple submissions.

Do you have a partner? If so, you're one step ahead of those who don't, at least as far as finding a guest appearance spot. This is especially true if

Dancers find small companies, such as Vermont Ballet Theatre, to dance with on lay-off. Annette Maynard and Mark Yin of Ballet Iowa in Vermont. © Yves Labbe.

You have an even better chance of guesting if you have a partner and if you've prepared a pas de deux. Michelle Pratt and Frank Dellapola. © Ralph J. Carbo, Jr.

you've worked on various pas de deux together while with your present company or if you can offer to rehearse the required repertoire even before you arrive for the guest spot. But note this: if the regional or junior company is doing its own choreography of a ballet classic such as *Sleeping Beauty* or *Midsummer Night's Dream,* you must be a quick study. Prepare yourself for this—seek a video of the choreography before you arrive, if possible. Review what you know of the classical ballet so that when you are faced with the new choreography, you'll have a firm basis to understand the differences.

So you arrive, you're the guest artist, and you've prepared yourself for the repertoire. At this point the most important thing is . . . *conduct yourself in a highly professional way!* This means:

• Be ready to rehearse when needed.

• Take company class with the dancers quietly and without appearing to be a prima donna.

• If you find you need extra warm-up time, do it quietly before class.

- Be prepared to attend costume fittings promptly, and if you are being supplied with shoes and tights, make sure you have sent sizes and specifications well in advance.
- Determine—ahead of time—from the shoe person in your company whether you can buy needed shoes before you go on layoff. *Or,* arrange for the company you are guesting with to buy them for you.
- You have been clear about your fee and whether your transportation, room, and board will have been paid. *As a guest artist you are entitled to this!*

And remember: Most regional and junior companies don't have funds to pay guest artists for long periods. Don't expect to fill in the blanks of your entire layoff period with one guest spot. Be grateful even if it's just one performance.

So, keep looking around.

How about teaching during layoff? Remember that teacher who nurtured you through those awkward, never-to-be-satisfied years, training you to be where you are today?

"I'm on layoff for three months," you tell her.

"I do hope you've *prepared*."

You ask whether she teaches class through the summer.

"Are you coming home, then? Of course you can take class here, though there's really nothing advanced enough for you, I'm afraid."

"I mean to teach, can I, could I . . . ?"

Dance teachers love to have a successful former student return to teach in their studio. It provides complete affirmation of the teacher's ability and her young students' hopes. What better public relations than to show off a former student who is now a professional and who *wants* to return to the scene of her early training. Young students will see it as a link to an ultimate professional career, and their parents will see it as confirmation that their little ones are in the right hands. Everybody's happy.

What if you've never taught? Who better to guide you through the first few steps than your former teacher? And besides, you've been taking class and working with ballet teachers for a dozen years or more, wouldn't you think that some of those techniques would rub off? Remember, too, you will probably be given the most basic, the easiest classes to work with, and as a professional there should be no mystery in showing others how to do such things.

What to do, then, and what to expect?

- Send your teacher—and any other ballet school you know and might wish to work in—photos and reviews of your work. (Sometimes teachers will want to provide these to the local media, announcing your guest teaching appearance.)

- Ask the teacher what should be conveyed to the students, refresh your memory on her syllabus, have the music for combinations and barre exercises worked out in advance.

- Be prepared to talk to the students about how you got into the company and what life is like in a professional company.

- Be positive about your experiences; understand that the young student will look at you with awe.

- When teaching, don't show off or make the work too difficult.

- Keep the classes clear and simple and slightly below the assigned level so that the students will feel good about themselves.

- Share anecdotes about your experiences after class.

Teaching during layoff can be rewarding from at least two perspectives: it gives you a chance to keep active and in shape during those down months—to say nothing about getting paid for it!—and it gives you an idea about yourself and the possibility of teaching once your ballet performance career is finished. Maybe you'll like it more than you think; maybe the future—way off, years away—might look clearer than it has in a long time.

Somewhat akin to teaching is a position as a work-study counselor at one of the summer ballet programs which exist in many parts of the country, such as Chatauqua, New York; Aspen, Colorado; Carlisle, Pennsylvania; and Boston, Massachusetts. The best time to begin searching is in January and February when the artistic director is on audition tour or is holding local auditions. Write to the summer program for an audition schedule and plan to audition when the director is close to your city. Then, when auditioning, make sure the director knows you are a professional looking for summer opportunities. The chances are there won't be much compensation involved, but there are other benefits. For example, at Burklyn Ballet Theatre in Vermont, free tuition to the summer program is offered to successful candidates (merely because you're a professional doesn't mean you'd be accepted for any particular program). In return you work in the dorms as a counselor or backstage with the production staff but

. . . you take all the classes and dance in all the performances. The major benefit, though, is that you are usually cast in lead roles, something only the principal dancer in your professional company gains. You have a chance to learn and perform at a level that would be impossible for you now in your professional company.

The point is this: as a work-study counselor you would dance, take class, perform, learn, and hone your technique while spending time away from the rigors of your full-time job. In a sense it is a busman's holiday, but in a sense, too, it is a major change of pace, and which of us doesn't need that from time to time?

Sometimes layoff doesn't mean going anywhere. Stay right where you are, stay with your friends and co-workers. In the larger ballet companies the costume and production staff work throughout the layoff time, preparing costumes and sets for the coming season. Have you ever thought you might like to try some of this work? It may be another way to prepare yourself for those sad days when your ballet performance career has to end. Talk to the company costumer and the production manager, see if there are any positions available as stitchers, carpenters, painters. Ask what the public relations staff might be up to during this time; see if they might not be able to use you as the upcoming season begins to fall in place. You might be good at meeting with groups and presenting the company well, or you might have a talent for layout and design or the written word.

The point is: merely because dancers are on layoff doesn't mean everyone in the company stops everything. Plans must always be made, one season must connect with another, so there will always be some company personnel who are working while you are on layoff. Find out who they are; think about what they do and whether you might find that work interesting. The results could surprise you.

There are lots of possibilities for managing layoff time. The several choices listed here are perhaps the most ballet-intensive, but they aren't exclusive. Think about other options: summer stock, for example, where musical theatre performances always need dancers; teaching swimming or running a bicycle tour which will keep you in fine shape for the new season; waitressing; returning to school. The list is as endless as your imagination can devise, but the one thing to remember is this: managing layoff time means that the emphasis should not only be on "layoff"—you must "manage" that time as well.

"I've got three months off!" you tell your former teacher.

"Think of all the things you can do with the time," she answers.

NONPERFORMANCE RESPONSIBILITIES

If people would come up to you, it would be much easier.
—Frank, a male dancer, Ballet Iowa

Most dancers understand that their company responsibilities extend outside the theatre. It isn't enough to arrive for your performance, apply your makeup, slip into your costume, warm up, then do your performance and flee the theatre and the company within an hour. Day in, day out, performance after performance, no company could survive if this was the sum total of effort.

There are definite outside responsibilities every dancer must carry, for and on behalf of the company. Call them nonperformance responsibilities if you wish (though they aren't quite that limiting), but they are real, they are expected, and they are important.

"Remember the reception after the show!" the production manager might remind you. It's not idle conversation. It's late, you're tired from the performance, but somehow you pull yourself together because receptions are the occasion for you to meet your audience, your board of directors, your fellow ballet supporters. As one artistic director put it, "It's the time when the money people meet the dance people," and the congeniality that develops will pay strong dividends for you and your company.

"I don't want to go!" you say? Well, check your contract. The chances are you'll be required to attend some of these events. And it really isn't so bad. For many nonperformers, you have celebrity status, you are important, you have just performed on stage! How many of them would love to do that? How many of them *could* do that? Sure, they might ask you silly questions or make inane comments ("How do you stay so slim?" "Doesn't all that dancing make you tired?") but it's all intended to admire what you do and how you do it. Money people feel important when they meet dancers. They are envious of you—though most won't admit it—because they would like to do what you do but can't. By staying congenial, you allow them to enjoy their importance.

Some dancers love receptions, of course, because in their own way the receptions become an extended performance, to say nothing of the fine food and sometimes elegant surroundings by which the reception host expects to be judged. Obviously, on tour, you will be the guests of the performance presenters, and since you are from out of town—and will, no doubt, judge them by comparison with other tour-stop receptions—you can expect some special attention. If you attend a reception in your home city, the presenter—even if it is your own board of directors—will certainly offer an affair that makes everyone smile and indulge themselves. It is simple human nature.

You, not surprisingly, will benefit. And how! Here's what lovely, dark-haired Lisa, currently with the Princeton Ballet, says, and it's easy to see she's a dancer who loves receptions. "All that great food, those friendly faces. Champagne and caviar, accolades. People looking at you, talking with you as if you were someone magic." She has not the slightest concern that the performance may not have gone well. "If they didn't like the performance, most aren't going to be at the reception; of course, if they *do* come, they aren't going to tell you you were awful, anyway."

Receptions, though, are a necessary part of a dancer's life, even if, for some, it becomes another act in the evening ballet program . . . this time with different costumes, different shoes, makeup, and hairstyle. The set may be a congenial party scene, but you are still in your role, and you are still performing. Your work day has not ended.

For the nondancers, the reception is a time to penetrate the footlights and discover the human being inside the make-believe. It's a time when the public can show admiration on a more personal basis for your work and

Dignitaries visit backstage with dancers of Les Grands Ballet Canadiens in Tokyo. © Deirdre Kelly.

when informal appreciation can be given to your company and the director.

Receptions perform another task as well. This is a good time to attract new contributors, to reach money people. Perhaps it's someone who has never been to the ballet, never actually met a professional dancer; or someone who has just moved to town and is a balletomane; or someone who has just acquired a big job, big responsibility . . . and big money! They see you, they talk to you, maybe even laugh with you, and they realize the company is not composed of still photos, costumed unreachables, and graceful, patterned bodies.

You are real! You breathe, you laugh, and you talk.

Receptions make you human to nondancers, and the importance should be obvious. The more the money people find to like about you, the more your salary—and the company—will benefit.

Doesn't it make you feel better, too, when you can be seen as a human being and not some fragile object that shouldn't be touched? Receptions make this happen; they can break down that wall of reserve and uncertainty between dancer and nondancer. "I love to have all those people watching me on stage," says pretty, green-eyed Pamela who recently toured with Ballet de Montréal, "especially when I have a solo. But I hate it when they expect me to be a china doll off stage." Then she feels like an object, and she resents the dehumanizing effect.

You breathe, you laugh, and you talk. Receptions make others aware of that, and you and the company become the beneficiaries. "Receptions are wonderful," adds dark-haired, quiet-spoken Emily, remembering her marathon two-month tour with the Nevada Dance Company. "You spend days eating in diners, and then suddenly you get a chance to dress up, eat elegant food, and meet intelligent and sophisticated people. It's just great!"

She's quiet for a moment.

"Receptions *are* wonderful," she repeats.

Then there are the dance critics, the ones who preview and write about dance for the media. You might meet them at a reception. You could see them walk through the studio door just as you miss an arabesque. You might make small talk with them outside the artistic director's office right after a horrendous rehearsal. The point is that dance critics hover about the ballet world, and you cannot program them as you would a sympathetic balletomane.

Dealing with dance critics is something every young dancer should become familiar with. The most important thing to remember is that dance critics write with their eyes, not their ears. It is what they *see* on stage, not what they *hear* from a publicity-minded artistic director or what they're told by a self-promoting dancer, that counts. For this reason critics can be remote and seem uninvolved in a conversation with you. But even so, the chances are you are being measured—height, bone structure, coloring—for the role or roles you have been or will be dancing. They might ask why or how you do a certain move, but it's more to understand the ballet than to provide special kudos for you.

And don't make the mistake of assuming that this soft, pudgy human being who calls himself a dance critic could not possibly know enough because—his flabby body as evidence—it's apparent he has never danced. To be a successful dance critic one has to *love* dance, to be obsessed with it. It isn't important whether the critic has danced professionally (there are many critics who have never danced). The dance critic writes *about* dance; he or she needn't *do* dance. The critic is the audience, what he or she sees is what the audience sees or should see. The dance critic does not write for you or other young dancers, though of course your skills and technique will be judged by how the dance critic measures you. But the dance critic is only interested in you as a tool to describe the art of ballet; it is to the audience that your work must have meaning.

Dance critics are the bridge between what dancers try to communicate to the audience and what the audience expects to receive. They translate, they interpret, they judge, and they sentence. The critic provides insights to the audience and offers an outside assessment to the dancers. Critics are to dance and ballet what the Good Housekeeping Seal is to consumer products or a medical discharge certificate is to an injured dancer. In simplest form, critics represent an outside, objective judgment on how well you dance and on how well your company performs.

Because their views are read by thousands, even hundreds of thousands, critics are important to dancers. Sometimes careers hang in the balance over a dance review, so companies go out of their way to treat dance critics with deference.

Some would argue though that not all dance critics are entitled to such respect. Rochelle Zide Booth, for instance. "The best ones are the ones who truly love dance, the ones who would attend everything whether they are critics or not," she says, offering the example of Walter Terry, late critic extraordinaire of the *Daily News*. But she considers him part of the old school. "Now we have critics who have spent months at critics' conferences and have learned their trade by reviewing experimental works in summer workshops. There's merit in that, but the point of reference is narrow." She compares the current state of dance criticism to that of an art critic who appreciates the genius of Picasso and Chagall but has no interest in Rembrandt or Renoir because they are premodern and hence of little current significance. Too superficial, she thinks, not learned enough. And she compares it to the dance world. It's like "people who admire the brilliance of Tish Brown and dismiss the genius of a golden oldie such as Martha Graham." A good critic, she thinks, should have equal knowledge of and appreciation for both.

A good critic should also be treated with courtesy. These are people who seek to make a living out of dance, too, and you should never assume they have any less love for the art form than you do. Nor should you assume they cannot write a dance review without speaking to the performers. Note the words of Valerie Sudol, dance critic for the *Newark* (N.J.) *Star Ledger:* "I never talk to the dancers," she says. "The only information I want from them is what they convey from the stage. My first responsibility is to my readers, not to the dancers or their company or their artistic director."

The critic *is* the audience. The critic writes for the readers, not for the dancers.

On the other hand, a dancer always searches for a good review, so critics become important for that reason alone. Respect is the key word: treat the critic as you would treat yourself. Be courteous, be considerate . . . and hope to see all of this returned.

As Rochelle Zide Booth experienced some years ago when she was with the Joffrey Ballet: "We were opening in Washington state, and I was dancing the Peasant pas de deux. I got the worst review I ever had, and the director told me it was because the local dance critic disliked my partner. The next year we returned to the same place, and I got, with my new partner, the most glowing review from the same critic! Obviously, I couldn't go to the newspaper and seek an explanation, but what I did do was write a note to the editor. I enclosed the [first] review with a note that said, 'Thank you for the positive reinforcement for an emerging dancer.' "

Will this dance critic remember her? Wouldn't you remember her if you received such a note? And wouldn't you look forward to her next performance?

A simple matter of respect and courtesy.

Along with the critics you must also contend with press photographers, and you should never assume these people know much about dance. They are professional photographers, not professional *dance* photographers.

They photograph sports, political rallies, labor incidents, automobile accidents, anything, in fact, that an editor considers news. You will most likely be photographed in the studio before the premier of a new ballet or before you go on tour or perhaps at the beginning of the season. You are "news," at least for that moment. But don't expect them to make you look your best. These are not specialized dance photographers.

And don't wear "junk" during these sessions either. No leg warmers, no tattered warm-up suits, T-shirts, plastic pants. A photographer, with the click of a shutter, can destroy the ethereal beauty and the clean line that you have worked so hard to achieve and which you hope the audience will remember. Generally, your artistic director or the company public relations department will let you know when press photographers are coming to the studio, and you can dress accordingly.

Remember this: outside of performances, the major contact between you and your audience is the press and the press photographer. How you come across may determine people's enthusiasm for watching you perform.

Things are different, though, when there is a photo call. At this specially designated photo opportunity, the photographer is a professional *dance* photographer and you and other members of the company are posing for the express purpose of calling attention to yourselves. There's no concept of "news" in all of this. A photo call is an opportunity for the company to acquire fine glossies for a number of uses throughout the year, and your responsibility is to prepare well and present yourself in the best way.

Here, things are more carefully done, and you have—or should have—the chance to pick your poses. You will want to think about all of this ahead of time, so you can be definite when you meet with the photographer. You must realize that—unlike the news story or quick magazine piece—photos that result from photo calls could be around for years. They may follow you from company to company. Think of it! This year's photo-call photos will certainly be in the latest program (this is often why they are taken); they could grace sandwich boards by the theatre entrance, especially on performance nights; they could accompany your résumé and tapes when you seek a new job. These photos are what the public will see, and you must be careful.

Photo calls can be scheduled outside the photographer's studio—on location, even in the dance studio. But the important thing is to see yourself as a performer and to establish how best you come across. Immaculate makeup and carefully coiffed hair are essential, and you should *always* leave your junk behind. Otherwise you might be tempted to put

The PR department may pick a sylvan glade to photograph a ballet such as Peter and the Wolf. *Vermont Ballet Theatre. © Yves Labbe.*

A performance shot can be used for your résumé. Susan Stowe, Ballet Metropolitan.

something on solely because it may have sentimental value, but its general effect may be to destroy the very image you are attempting to project.

Remember this, too: photos taken of you during these photo calls become the property of your company. They can do with them as they wish, and you have little to say about it, so long as the photos are in any way connected to your job.

The company is paying the photographer, so your rights are severely limited; after all, you are gaining the benefit of whatever publicity value might be generated. There really isn't much you can do under these circumstances, except to glory in whatever publicity gains come your way.

Sometimes the consequences can be unnerving. A few years ago the public relations director of a major ballet company walked into the studio, assembled the dancers, and asked, "Would anyone like to make extra money this weekend?" A downtown photographer wanted to shoot two dancers in costume—one female, one male; one in tutu, one as a cavalier.

Two dancers raised their hands, and they were directed to the wardrobe department, where they chose their costumes. The next day the shoot went well; the dancers signed a standard release form and were paid. Some weeks later they even received a note of thanks from the photographer and a single 8 × 10 glossy of themselves.

They were delighted.

But some years later the photograph of the female dancer appeared on a city billboard advertising a Forty-second Street massage parlor!

"What can I do?" the dancer cried, seeking immediate legal help.

"Nothing, I'm afraid," was the response from her lawyer. "The photo call was legitimate; you signed the release; you were paid; the photo and the rights to its distribution and reproduction belonged to the photographer."

"But I didn't know . . ." the dancer started to say.

"Be more careful," was her lawyer's response. Ask what the photo will be used for, discover whether the photo call is at the instigation of the company, and find out who will own the photos once the shoot is finished.

Photo calls can certainly take you far from the theatre, but there are times when far away is simply too far. Ask and understand your rights to these photos. Then you will be protected.

Joining a Foreign   6
Company

They contract you for twelve months, pay you for
thirteen months, and you get holiday pay too!
                    —David Howard, master teacher

The lure of the Continent . . . or is it Down Under? Below the
    equator? The Far East?
        There are ballet companies throughout the world, and for a young
dancer, these companies provide opportunities that few professions offer.
Think of it! To travel *and* to dance! Live in a foreign country, dance in a
foreign country, learn a foreign culture . . . all these things, and more, are
possible if you cast your eyes beyond the boundaries of the United States.

American dancers do join foreign companies, in fact they've been doing
it for many years. There are even some American artistic directors of
foreign companies. Ballet is not a nationalistic art form; it crosses borders
as easily as the air we breathe. (Although state-funded ballet companies
may be required to hire citizens of the country—Britain is one example.
Alexander Bennett, former principal with the Royal Ballet, confirms it
sadly. "It used to be that if you could prove you had one British parent," he
says, "they could accept you, but that has changed.") Artistic directors
want talent not political conformity or ethnic similarity, and it matters
little—except to the state funded companies—that a dancer carries papers
from some other country.

The only thing that matters is talent. Are you good enough, trainable
enough? Foreign companies want you if you are.

Do you have that spirit of adventure which propels you to wonder what
it would be like to live elsewhere? Are you curious enough to give it serious
thought? Are you self-confident enough to know you can handle most
things in a strange culture?

Yes! yes! you answer, and so you begin to plan.

Ask yourself seven questions:
- What countries do I want to go to?
- Which cities in those countries have ballet companies?
- How big are those companies?
- Do these companies tour?
- Who is the artistic director?
- Do they use live or taped music?
- Do they have a resident theatre?

This information—all of it—is your *Stern's Performing Arts Guide,* which by now has a certain dog-eared quality to it. (You may want to purchase an updated edition.) Flip to the "Foreign Ballet Companies" section and read, read, read.

Then, sit down and write a letter. Write many letters, in fact, because your chances of landing a job suffer the same odds as they do in the United States: there are infinitely more dancers looking for work than work looking for dancers. Make your letter personal. (Remember the old days when you were looking for your first apprenticeship? Do it the same way.) Address your letter to the artistic director. (Write it in English, of course, unless you know another language and feel comfortable writing in that language.) And enclose your résumé and photographs.

Your letter should say that you want work in _____ (name the locale—Europe, South America, Australia, etc.). Ask when the company will be in the United States and where you could audition for them. Or, could you audition at their home studio, and when would that be convenient. The unfortunate part of this last suggestion is that you may be forced to travel to *them,* and it's going to cost you! No one is reimbursed for coming to an audition, even if you have been invited, so you might have to bear plane costs, meal and hotel costs, even some unforeseen shoe costs.

Is it worth it? Only you can really tell because only you know how much you want to join this company, and only you know what sacrifices you are willing to make.

But note this: you'll get more replies to your letter than you would have from companies in the United States. Foreign companies are known for responding, even if it's a negative response; they are much more reliable about this sort of thing than are United States companies.

Now for the big money alternative. You can—some do—make an audition *tour* of a foreign locale, setting up a series of auditions ahead of time. Need we say this will be expensive? But it has the advantage of not putting most of your ballet tights in one laundry basket. You are spreading your risk and increasing your chances of landing a job. It shouldn't be done, however, on the spur of the moment . . . "Hi! I'm in the area, may I come in and audition?" This doesn't work in a foreign company setting any better than it would work here. You *must* set up your audition tour in advance, well in advance, and you shouldn't book your ticket until you have something in writing from the companies that they will provide you an audition. Remember, customs in each country differ, and you should not expect any less formality than you are used to here.

Sometimes international competitions can open the door to foreign company auditions. Suppose you enter one. It's certain there will be foreign company representatives—even artistic directors—in attendance, and you now have them in a position where they will be watching you. There are several things you should do before the competition:

- Find out from the official roster which directors are attending.

- Find out from the registration desk where they are staying.

- Write a polite note saying you are interested in the company and would like to audition.

- If you are competing, tell where and when.

- If you are simply taking class, tell where and when and whose classes you are taking.

- Provide a number and/or an address where you will be staying and how long you will be staying.

Look at it this way . . . you will be doing the director a favor by offering yourself at a time and a place which is convenient for him and for you. He doesn't have to set the audition, and you don't have to make a special trip to present yourself. You perform, he watches. Simple.

And, of course, if you do happen to win a medal at the competition, your worries are over. Chances are you will be able to choose your company as there will be more than one artistic director lining up outside your door. Mary Day, of the Washington Ballet, tells the story of Amanda McKerrow, a seventeen-year-old dancer she took to the International Ballet Competition in Moscow a few years ago. "I said we are going for the experience of it," she remembers. "I said it will be a wonderful trip with lots of international dancers, something we can enjoy. We went thinking we were only going for the fun and experience, and it came as a tremendous surprise when we won a gold medal." She pauses. "I would say it was the most exciting incident in my life."

For Amanda McKerrow, too. Don't you think the directors vied with one another to have her in their company? Seventeen years old. The foreign company presence in Moscow must have been substantial.

That's the way to pick and choose the company you want!

There is another alternative, of course, if you seek to be seen by a foreign company director: study in the company-affiliated school for a summer or even an entire school year, if you can afford it. Make your mark in the classes, and wait to be seen . . . but it can be a long wait, unless you show something special or have a fortuitous audition. This is a roundabout method of gaining the AD's attention, but it has worked for some—so long as patience doesn't wear out! The one advantage here is that the longer you remain in the school the more familiar you become with the company, the repertoire, the artistic director, and the kind of dancer sought. When an opening in the company comes up, the director may find it much easier to look to the school than to search outside.

But there are no guarantees here. You know that.

And, of course, joining the foreign company school means you must plan and budget just as if you are joining the foreign company itself. The culture, the language, the people—all new, all strange. It will still take an adventurous soul to handle it easily.

The welcome letter comes, finally. You have been accepted—you are offered a job with a foreign company. What's the first step?

Make sure you have a valid passport!

Without a passport you won't be allowed to enter that foreign country, unless it's Canada. Even there, however, you can't work without special approval. So, passport or not, you must obtain a work permit, and to get this your passport should be photocopied and notarized and sent to the company manager. First!

Remember, without the work permit, you can't work. So get that passport copy out fast, let the company manager apply for your work permit, and hope it happens without delay. You can assume that if the foreign company wants you, they'll do everything in their power to get you that work permit quickly. As international ballet veteran Alexander Bennett says: "If they want you, they'll move mountains to get you."

Generally, the work permit is for one year, with an option for the company to renew it (you don't renew; the company does). For as long as you work in a foreign setting you will need this—or some other—work permit, and you must be able to show it when requested.

Of course, if you decide to become a citizen of the country and relinquish your current citizenship, the work permit rules don't apply. Then you acquire the rights of a citizen, and that will certainly subject you to different rules.

But assuming you wish to retain your citizenship, you can expect to wait a short while before your work permit comes through (sometimes it can take up to three months, depending on the country bureaucracy). Remember, until the work permit comes through, you cannot work . . . but there are a few other things you should do. Foremost, perhaps, is to buy yourself a decent Walkman and an audio course in the language of the country your company calls home. Listen and learn as much as you can; practice pronunciation and the simpler phrases; become familiar with menu items and directions. Read a guidebook on the country; study the geography and the place names.

Don't do what Alexander Bennett did at an early stage in his career: "I went to Brazil [a Portuguese-speaking country] thinking my limited knowledge of Spanish would help," he recalls. "Actually it was a hindrance. When I had to converse in Portuguese, it was easier to forget the Spanish. The right translations were really hard. I remember when I went into my apartment and was told to turn on the water at a specific time because there was a shortage. One morning I woke with a flood on the floor. I had been turning the water on instead of off—everything was opposite!"

One thing you'll notice if you join a European company is how strong a part of the arts scene the ballet world is. Open a guidebook, read about the country and its cities in the encyclopedia, and often you'll find that the company and its resident theatre are listed as one of the premier attractions. In Europe a city's ballet company is on a par with a U.S. city's major league baseball team. Both provide residents with pride; both offer a closely supported spectacle.

"It's always amazes me," says internationally renowned ballet teacher David Howard, "that the tram driver knows what is being performed and who is performing with the local ballet company at the Opera House." It could be the local florist, just as easily, or the local beautician or the local grocery store clerk. The point is that the local ballet company is a general source of pride. "Everyone has an interest in the theatre," Howard says, pointing out that in Europe, theatres are often a part of beautiful old buildings whose history also provides local people with an added sense of importance. Dance in America can't compete with all of this, and David Howard shakes his head sadly: "We perform in civic centers, and they can be so ugly."

Foreign companies, though, operate with contracts just as we do here. If you are accepted, the language of the contract will *not* be English (unless of course you're joining the Royal Ballet or Australian National Ballet). Get a translation of the contract so you are completely familiar with what's expected from you and what you should expect from the company.

Get that contract translated! Try your local high school, college, even your travel agent. Failing this get in touch with a local German club or French club or Spanish club or . . . well, you get the idea.

Even if the translation is a bit rough, you are better off knowing as much as you can about the people you will be spending at least next year with. This doesn't mean you should worry about who these people are. If the company is well known, and especially if it is supported by the government, you should have nothing to worry about. If it's a smaller, less well-known company, you might get in touch with your local arts council and they could check it out for you. This group donates its time to help artists, and you should certainly qualify.

Let's assume you are ready to join a company in Europe. What differences can you expect between your European and American experiences? First of all (and this is one that many American dancers rave about) your contract is not for twenty-six or thirty-nine weeks, but for the entire year! Many European companies pay biweekly, so you have twenty-six pay periods a year, a full year's employment, not just seasonal employment!

Included, too, is a vacation period—sometimes as long as eight weeks. You're not on layoff, you're on paid vacation. You are employed throughout the year.

Benefits are part of the package: free medical care, pension plan plus a social security program. You pay some of this cost, of course, but so does the company. It can add up quickly. David Howard tells of an American dancer who recently retired from the Basel (Switzerland) Ballet Company after only ten years. "When you leave the country you can take your pension money with you," he says, "so she walked away with more than 60,000 francs [about $45,000]." He also mentions that France has an equally generous plan. "Dancers have to retire there at forty," he adds, and it's understood that retirement is no financial burden to the dancer.

You are ready to go now. Your contract is signed, your passport and visa are in hand, your flight is booked, you are learning the language, you've read all you can about the country and city, and you can even find it on the map! You are attending class daily to keep in shape. All you have to do is . . . pack.

A simple tip: pack enough clothes plus your favorite dance clothes to last six weeks. No more. Once you are settled, you can always add or subtract what you need or can do without. Six weeks' worth is really enough.

If you need more than this, have friends or family send it via air cargo. Check the yellow pages for companies that ship out of the country, and make arrangements with them ahead of time. Once you settle in, your friends or family can send the rest of your things.

Not long after you arrive, you should fall quickly into the familiar routine. There are bound to be some English-speaking dancers in the company who will answer such questions as "Where do I stand at the barre?" "How do I know which rehearsal to attend?"

There will be some changes from what you are used to, however. "In the Royal Ballet," says Alexander Bennett, "we had separate classes for men and women at ten and ten-thirty, then we broke for lunch, and then we had rehearsal from two-thirty to five in the afternoon. We never rehearsed in the evening."

But David Howard says that "in Basel they have class at ten, work until two, then break from two to five in the afternoon. They return to rehearse from five to eight in the evening." There's a reason for this strange schedule in Basel. "If they didn't have this afternoon break, they would never have any time to do their shopping because everything closes at six. They work around the environment."

So you arrive at the studio, excited, ready to go to work. First day, everything new, in a strange country, wondering . . . and here comes your first surprise!

The studio floor is raked!

A little later you walk into the theatre, and here the *stage* is raked!

You're used to a flat floor and a flat stage. That's all there is in the United States. Alexander Bennett laughs as he remembers: "The thing that bothered me, though it never seemed to bother the Europeans, was the stage; it was always so heavily raked." Studio or theatre, it didn't matter, they are raked to match one another. "When you go to daily class, you have to walk uphill to get to the barre," he laughs, then adds, "it tends to put your weight on your heels, and this could be the reason why European training is inclined to keep dancers on their heels rather on the front of their feet as we do over here."

Dancing with a foreign company has its exotic side, to be sure. But reality can sometimes temper anyone's enthusiasm. For example, "American dancers are often appalled by the shared showering facilities and bathrooms in Europe," says Alexander Bennett. "It's not unheard of to have only one or two bathrooms backstage for the cast and all the backstage staff!"

Life with a foreign company is different, not necessarily better or worse. You should understand the differences even as you enjoy the life. Here are some young dancers' typical reactions to a first year in a foreign company:

• "The food is different, so heavy, and there aren't enough salads—no salad dressings to speak of." (Member of the Scottish-American Ballet)

• "I miss being able to call home every other day and not being able to get home for a week's layoff. My family likes it, though, because now they have an excuse to visit." (Member of a ballet company in France)

• "Do you know I've never had a review in English? It's not the same even if it's translated into English." (Member of a ballet company in Holland)

Could these problems overwhelm you? The dancers themselves never gave a thought to leaving their foreign companies. They simply expressed the fact that there are certain things one must adjust to. The foreign company experience can be exciting and rewarding, even if it might be a bit unsettling at times.

But it's where those forever memories come from, and the balance is clearly in the foreign company's favor.

So . . . get out your atlas, choose a country you wish to live in, and take the first step . . .

Professional Development 7

*I think many times when we get involved with the
profession, the craft of dancing, we forget why we came
into it—because we love it and we're passionate about it.*
—Richard Englund, artistic director, Joffrey II

ou've been in the same company for three years, having joined
after an apprenticeship. This was, and still is, the company of your
dreams. But occasionally the sameness of daily class seems boring.
Will it always be like this? You are getting better parts, being used in
most performances, your growth seems to be assured, but the sparkle isn't
always there.

An artist, any artist, needs variety to grow, and that's what you are, an
artist.

A dancer remembers her childhood:

> My parents moved to a romantic island off the coast of France
> when I was eight. They had gone ahead to prepare our new home.
> They picked me up at the airport, and I well remember the drive
> home. The sea was crystal blue reflecting a cloudless sky, the beach
> golden, and the bullrushes along the dunes swayed with silver
> blooms. It was the most beautiful place I had ever been to.
>
> But five years later I realized that the island didn't shine with the
> brilliance of newness. Nothing had changed—it was an everyday
> scene in my eyes now, and I just wasn't seeing all the things that
> had impressed me.

That combination of steps which seemed so challenging when you
joined the company is no longer difficult or new. You've mastered the
uniqueness of your ballet master. He knows the best way to warm up his
dancers, quickly and efficiently, and how to feed the special needs of each
one.

To grow as an artist you need to look outside the narrow confines of
your company and into the depths of yourself.

What inspires you?

Perhaps class with a new teacher? Or the quiet solitude of an art gallery? Maybe the splendor of a mountain range? An evening at home listening to new music, or watching a video of a dancer interpret a role you dance or hope to dance?

Or maybe a child's innocent acceptance of what you can share as a teacher could help you grow as a dancer.

All of these related arts are easily found. Remember Richard Englund's words about his dancers in Greece: "Some of those dancers will never be quite the same."

Whenever there is a master teacher in the area, try to take the class. You can find out about classes by contacting area studios and asking to be put on their mailing lists.

And when you are on tour try to take classes in professional schools. Often a teacher in the smallest town can give you new insights into technique and artistry.

The solitude of a fine art gallery can renew your spirits and inspire your next performance. From the gentle hues of Monet's soaring poplar trees, the disciplined poise of a Degas, the gentle cascade of hair in Jansem's

Teaching beginners is a great reminder of technique fundamentals and a helpful source of income. Patricia Whitehill. © Susan Hoyt von Trapp.

Arabesque, or the stark lines of a Picasso, you can find inspiration in just the way such artists inspired Diaghilev's choreographers and artists at the beginning of the century.

Or the passion of Rodin's sculpture. What does *The Kiss* say to you? How can you utilize another artist's vision in your artistic growth?

George Balanchine grew up immersed in the Russian traditions of Petipa, Tchaikovsky, Jules Perrot, and Adolphe Adam, and his choreography was inspired by moderns such as Stravinsky, Picasso, and Chagall. Is there a doubt his ultimate work will live forever?

Dance history is fascinating too.

"History," you exclaim, "so boring."

Not so. What you do today comes directly from history. For example, dancers were "flying" as early as 1796; scenery moved realistically in 1647. Taglioni, that nineteenth-century superstar, had a steel rose on stage to put her toe into, giving her unprecedented balance in the air.

Do you love the intrigue of a Danielle Steele novel? Read of the intrigues in Diaghilev's Ballet Russe de Monte Carlo, in S. L. Grigoriev's *The Diaghilev Ballet*.

Love true-life adventure? Try *Split Seconds* by Tamara Geva, which tells of the escape of Geva, Balanchine, and Danilova from Russia. Or Margot Fonteyn's autobiography, which details political escape, with husband Roberto de Arias, from a dictator-inspired death sentence in Panama.

Loyce Houlton, American choreographer emeritus, admonishes, "Look to architecture for inspiration." And certainly the soaring lines and port de bras of her ballet *Windsong* show her appreciation of Gothic arches and slender spires. Look at the way the dancers' arms arch together, or the way their bodies, during partnering, soar toward the sky.

But perhaps you would like to stay home and listen to music, watch television, or play with your cat. (Balanchine learned much from watching his cat leap.) Listen to different composers. Learn new movement from MTV dancers. (You never know when a new and innovative choreographer will ask you to execute an old step in a new way!) Review some of the tapes you used to devour—famous dancers dancing famous roles. Take *Romeo and Juliet* as an example. Watch the gentle innocence of a forty-five-year-old Fonteyn playing mandolin as the fifteen-year-old Juliet. Or the fluidity and joy of Alexandra Ferri in the balcony pas de deux, or Natalia Makarova's sensuality in the bedroom pas de deux. Draw from all of these stars to extend your own special qualities.

Even *Nutcracker* can take on special qualities if you have explored the art of Spanish, Chinese, or Middle Eastern dancing. Imagine your joy when a critic mentions your unique interpretation of one of these roles! Imagine your artistic director's reaction!

If it sounds as though you must spend every waking hour immersed in dance, you are not far off. More than any other artist (even a singer) you carry the tools of your art with you. You have no canvas, no violin, no

Acting technique is required in many dance roles. Maurice Lemay as Doctor Coppélius, Les Grands Ballets Canadiens. © Michael Slobodian.

paper or pen; you and your body are the instruments of your art. You can tune the instrument walking on a sandy beach or climbing a green mountain. You can exercise your neck sitting on a plane or stretch your feet in a supermarket line. (Even a singer can't practice here, at least not without attracting a certain amount of attention!)

You are a dancer—every moment of your career.

And now you are growing as an artist!

Appendices

SAMPLE RÉSUMÉ

MARY SMITH
(816) 555-1234

Age: 26
Height: 5'6"
Weight: 108 lbs.

Permanent Address:
700 Main Street
Kansas City, MO 64105
Seasonal Address:
145 W. 10th Street
NY, NY 10014

PROFESSIONAL EXPERIENCE
1988-89   Omaha Ballet Co.
1987-88   Ballet de Montréal (corps de ballet, soloist)
1985-87   Hartford Ballet Co. (apprentice)

TRAINING
1982-85   National Academy of the Arts
1980-82   Walnut Hill School
1976-80   Burklyn Ballet Theatre
1977-85   Burklyn Ballet Theatre Summer Program
1968-76   Shore Ballet School

ROLES DANCED
Soloist: Omaha Ballet and Hartford Ballet —Mirlitons
                (Nutcracker)
                Omaha Ballet—Arabian (Nutcracker)
                Ballet de Montréal—Snow Queen (See *Dance Magazine,*
                Dec. 1988)
Corps de Ballet: Omaha Ballet—Carmina Burana, Nutcracker, Coppélia
                Ballet de Montréal—Symphonie de Nouveau Monde,
                Facade, Requiem, Concertante
                Hartford Ballet—Allegro Brilliante, Nutcracker, Carmina
                Burana, Coppélia, New England Triptych
Pas de Deux: White Swan, La Bayadère, Don Quixote, Peasant pas de
                deux (Giselle), Paquita

AWARDS
1985 National Arts and Letters (Midwest region)
1986 National Academy of the Arts Dance Award

Enclosures: *Dance Magazine* 1985, 1988
Composite photograph

References and video tapes (VHS) upon request.

Dancer's Working Agreement and Addendum

The Atlanta Ballet
Dancer's Working Agreement

Individual Employment Agreement made and entered into this ___ day of _____, 19__, by and between The Atlanta Ballet, Inc., hereinafter called the "company" and _____, hereinafter called the "artist".

Witnesseth:

Whereas, the company and artist agree to the Mission Statement of The Atlanta Ballet as follows: The Atlanta Ballet's mission is to provide high quality dance entertainment and educational programs for the broadest number of people, and be a Company with a local and national reputation for high artistic standards, imagination and managerial excellence; and

Whereas, the company is engaged in the production of and presentation of ballet performances and desires to secure the professional services of the artist for the 19__–19__ season; and

Whereas, the artist desires to render such services unto the company upon the terms and conditions hereinafter set forth;

Now therefore, in consideration of the foregoing and of the stipulations and conditions herein contained and set forth, the parties hereto agree as follows:

I. Term of Employment

The company hereby engages and employs the artist as a dancer, and the artist hereby agrees to be so engaged and employed for a total period of __ weeks, beginning on _____, 19__ through _____, 19__, and _____, 19__ through _____, 19__, said term of artist's employment shall continue until specified time unless sooner terminated by one of the following conditions:

a) The death of the artist.

b) The complete disability of the artist. "Complete disability" as used herein shall mean the inability of the artist due to weight, illness, accident, or other physical or mental incapacity to perform the services provided for hereunder for an aggregate of fourteen (14) days within any period of thirty (30) consecutive days during the term hereof. The COMPANY may demand a certificate of a doctor as to the illness of the ARTIST and examination by a doctor as a condition precedent to sick leave.

c) When the ARTIST is engaged by the COMPANY, it is understood and agreed that in case of insubordination and/or alcohol or drug abuse during any Company function, the ARTIST is subject to immediate dismissal. In such an event, if the ARTIST is on tour, the COMPANY will provide payment for one-way transportation to the city of origination.

d) When the ARTIST is engaged by the COMPANY, it is understood and agreed that in the event of circumstances beyond the COMPANY's control, should the COMPANY not be able to maintain and/or continue its scheduled season, the COMPANY shall give the ARTIST a minimum of two (2) weeks notice of termination of employment.

e) When the ARTIST is engaged by the COMPANY, the COMPANY shall have the option to engage the ARTIST to render his/her services as a dancer for a specified period of consecutive employment beyond the terms of this contract. This option may be exercised by the COMPANY by delivering notice to the ARTIST _____ weeks prior to the completion of the initial employment set forth in the Agreement. This option may be finalized with specific dates by an Addendum to the original Agreement and initialed by the ARTIST and COMPANY, or by a new contract drawn up at the time by the COMPANY.

II. RULES AND REGULATIONS

a) When the ARTIST is engaged by the COMPANY, the ARTIST shall be subject to the direction of the Artistic Director, and those other persons whom the Artistic Director may empower with the authority to control the ARTIST, such as the Ballet Master/Mistress, choreographers, the Company Stage Manager, or other employees of the COMPANY.

b) When the ARTIST is engaged by the COMPANY, the ARTIST agrees to attend and take part in COMPANY directed daily class, rehearsals, dress rehearsals, performances, costume fittings, photo calls, and other services as the COMPANY may require.

c) When the ARTIST is engaged by the COMPANY, the ARTIST agrees to comply with all COMPANY regulations as provided for in the Basic Agreement between the Atlanta Ballet, Inc., and the Artist of The Atlanta

Ballet. The Basic Agreement currently in force is attached hereto and incorporated herein by reference, and by signing this Individual Employment Agreement, the ARTIST represents that he or she has read and understood the said Basic Agreement. The COMPANY shall provide the ARTIST with advance written notice of any mutually agreed upon changes and/or additions by the two said parties.

d) When the ARTIST is engaged by the COMPANY, the ARTIST shall not accept assignments to render any service to a third party during the period of his/her Individual Working Agreement, except as otherwise provided in the Basic Agreement.

III. COMPENSATION

In consideration of the ARTIST's performance of his/her duties and responsibilities hereunder, the COMPANY agrees to pay the ARTIST $_____ a week, payable bi-weekly. In addition to the salary herein provided, the COMPANY shall also provide Worker's Compensation Insurance, Unemployment Insurance, Social Security Insurance, and Health/Medical Insurance as provided in the Basic Agreement. The ARTIST understands that the COMPANY will deduct from his/her salary payments hereunder, all Income and Social Security Taxes as are required by Federal, State and Local Laws. The COMPANY shall also provide the ARTIST with_____ per diem as a food allowance and provide lodging for the ARTIST when the ARTIST is touring outside the city of origination.

IV. FORCE MAJEURE

It is agreed that if the COMPANY cannot perform because of fire, act of God, war, the public enemy or for any other cause of the same general class which could not be resonably anticipated or prevented, then the COMPANY shall notify the ARTIST thereof, and the ARTIST shall not be entitled to any individual contractual compensation for the time during which said services shall not, for such reason, or reasons, be rendered.

V.

This Individual Employment Agreement, including the Basic Agreement incorporated herein by reference (including changes and/or additions thereto pursuant to Paragraph I(e) and II(c) hereof), constitutes the entire Agreement between the COMPANY and the ARTIST. This Employment Agreement shall be interpreted in accordance with, and in all respects, governed by the Laws of the State of Georgia.

In witness whereof the parties have hereunder set their hands on the day and year first written above.

Atlanta Ballet, Inc.   Artist

_____   _____

Robert Barnett
Artistic Director

THE ATLANTA BALLET
ADDENDUM TO THE DANCER'S WORKING AGREEMENT

This addendum, when signed by both ARTIST and COMPANY, is hereby incorporated with the same force and effect into the DANCER'S BASIC AGREEMENT.

The following is an addition to Section III, Health and Medical Benefits, paragraph A1;

Health/medical insurance will take effect one month after Artist initially begins employment with Company.

Section III, paragraph A1 of the DANCER'S WORKING AGREEMENT will now read:

1) Company shall pay the total cost of health/medical insurance continuously and without interruption through the term of the Artist's Individual Working Agreement. Health/medical insurance will take effect one month after ARTIST intially begins employment with COMPANY. In the event that the COMPANY and the ARTIST have entered into an individual contract for the following season, prior to the expiration of current contract, the COMPANY shall provide and pay total cost of said insurance for the length of the interim between contracted employment periods.

ATLANTA BALLET, INC.   ARTIST

_____   _____

Robert Barnett
Artistic Director

The Hartford Ballet
Apprentice Contract

AGREEMENT is made this __ day of _____, 1989 by and between THE HARTFORD BALLET INCORPORATED, a Connecticut non-stock corporation with its principal place of business in the City of Hartford, County of Hartford, and State of Connecticut, hereinafter called the "Company," and _____ hereinafter called the "Apprentice."

1. *Duties:* The Company will engage _____ as an Apprentice for the term of this Contract stated below. The primary responsibility of the Apprentice is to his/her work with the Company. The Apprentice will be required to attend classes in the School of the Hartford Ballet's Advanced Summer Workshop and Certificate Program in Performance Preparation during the term of this Contract. The Apprentice will rehearse and perform in such dance productions as may be required by the Company and/or School and will at all times maintain the standards of the Company and School.

The Apprentice agrees to be bound by the terms and conditions of the Certificate Program in Performance Preparation as set forth in the Contract and Catalog of that Program (copies attached). In case of conflict this Apprentice Contract shall have precedence.

2. *Term:* The term of this Contract shall be from _____ through _____. The Apprentice will attend classes in the School on a full-time basis during all periods of Company layoff and will likewise take classes with the Company during School vacations, except when such vacations occur during Company layoffs.

3. *Stipend:* The Company will pay to the Apprentice a living stipend of _____ per month for __ months ONLY, to be paid in semi-monthly installments of $_____ on the 15th and the last day of each month, beginning _____ .

In addition, the Company will provide shoes (fifteen (15) pair of pointe shoes and four (4) pair of ballet slippers for women; fifteen (15) pair ballet slippers for men) and touring expenses as necessary for Company performances.

The Apprentice will receive a full scholarship, for all classes required by this Contract, for study in the Advanced Summer Workshop and the Certificate Program in Performance Preparation, as well as credit toward the School of the Hartford Ballet's Certificate in Dance Performance for Certificate Program classes and work with the Company.

In addition, the Apprentice is encouraged to apply for Federal Financial Aid as a student in the Certificate Program in Performance Preparation.

4. *Insurance:* In case of accident or injury resulting from performance of duties under this Contract, the Apprentice shall be covered by the School's Student Accident Insurance Policy, subject to the limitations and deductibles in effect at the time.

5. *Termination:* The Company may, upon request of the Artistic Director and School Director, terminate this Apprenticeship if the Apprentice fails to maintain the standards set by the Company and/or School.

If the Apprentice shall breach any terms of this Contract then the Company may, upon two (2) weeks written notice, terminate this contract.

Any desire by the Apprentice to terminate this Contract prior to _____ must be indicated in writing at least one (1) month prior to termination of the Contract.

6. *Covenant:* During the term of this Contract the Apprentice covenants and agrees not to perform technically or otherwise assist any other company or to use any dance material either directly or indirectly, independently, or as a member of any organization, without the written permission of the Company.

7. *Assignment:* This Contract shall inure to the benefit of and shall be binding upon the Company, its successors or assigns.

8. *Acceptance:* The Company shall have the option to suspend or cancel this Contract if it has not been duly signed and returned to the Company within ten (10) working days of the date first written above.

IN WITNESS WHEREOF, the parties have executed this Contract as of the day and year first written above.

For The Hartford Ballet, Inc.:   Agreed:

_____

_____

Apprentice Signature

_____

Apprentice Social Security Number

_____

Local Address

_____

_____

Phone

_____

Permanent Address

_____

_____

Phone

The Atlanta Ballet
Dancer's Basic Agreement

I. Agreement

WHEREAS, the Management and the Dancers of The Atlanta Ballet believe that it would be in the best interest of both parties to write down certain rules, regulations and conditions under which the Ballet will operate; and

WHEREAS, both parties agree that the overriding purpose of this Agreement is the enhancement of The Atlanta Ballet and the achievement of providing high quality dance entertainment and educational programs for the broadest number of people in Atlanta, Georgia, and the nation; and

WHEREAS, the foregoing is subject to the financial circumstances of The Atlanta Ballet and rehearsal, performance and personal exigencies;

NOW THEREFORE, and in consideration of the spirit of the foregoing and of the rules and regulations herein contained and set forth;

The Atlanta Ballet, Inc. (hereinafter called the COMPANY) and the Dancers of The Atlanta Ballet, Inc. (hereinafter called the ARTIST) agree that the provisions of the Agreement shall apply to all ARTISTS employed as Dancers in the COMPANY unless otherwise noted within. This Agreement made, executed and delivered in the City of Atlanta, county of Fulton and State of Georgia, this 13th day of May, 1988 by and between The Atlanta Ballet, Inc. and the Dancers of The Atlanta Ballet, Inc. covering the period from _____ through _____.

II. Worker's Compensation, Unemployment Insurance, and Social Security

A) The COMPANY must carry at its expense adequate Worker's Compensation Insurance (hereinafter "WCI") securing to all ARTISTS wherever they may work as Atlanta Ballet Dancers for The Atlanta Ballet, Inc., compensation for disability or death from injury arising out of and in the course of their employment without regard for compensation if the injury has been occasioned by intoxication or illegal drug use by the ARTIST while on duty, or by willful intention of the injured ARTIST to bring about the injury to him/herself. In an effort to reduce the COMPANY's WCI experience rating-based premium, each ARTIST shall truthfully and promptly report to the COMPANY all injuries and illnesses sustained on the job and further shall provide the COMPANY, if requested, an accurate written medical evaluation of his/her condition. The COMPANY agrees to hold a meeting with the ARTIST at the beginning of each season to explain procedures to follow when reporting a WCI claim.

B) The COMPANY agrees to obtain Unemployment Insurance coverage for all ARTISTS according to the Unemployment Laws of the State of Georgia.

C) The COMPANY agrees to cover all ARTISTS under the Social Security Law of the United States and to execute and file the necessary forms required to obtain such coverage and therefore, as required by law to make the proper contributions.

III. HEALTH AND MEDICAL BENEFITS

A) The COMPANY agrees to provide health/medical and dental insurance on behalf of ARTIST according to the following terms and conditions:

1) COMPANY shall pay the total cost of health/medical insurance continuously and without interruption through the term of the ARTIST's Individual Working Agreement. In the event that the COMPANY and the ARTIST have entered into an individual contract for the following season, prior to expiration of current contract, the COMPANY shall provide and pay total cost of said insurance for the length of the interim between contracted employment periods.

a) Health insurance for APPRENTICES is provided at the expense of the APPRENTICE. The current monthly premium is ____ and is subject to change when our insurance contract is renewed. The APPRENTICE wishing to be covered for health insurance, must notify the Business Office and the amount of the premium will be deducted from his/her paycheck.

2) Should ARTIST fail to return for the succeeding employment year, he/she shall be held accountable for the total reimbursement of any expenditures made for insurance premiums on his/her behalf by the COMPANY between periods of employment as this constitutes a legal debt to the COMPANY.

3) The COMPANY shall make available to ARTIST's family (as defined by insurance carriers) health/medical and dental insurance coverage through the COMPANY's insurance plans. ARTIST shall be responsible for the payment of any additional premium cost for family coverage over and above premium costs for ARTIST's basic coverage.

4) The COMPANY shall make available to ARTIST dental insurance at the option of the ARTIST. Premium for dental insurance shall be the responsibility of ARTIST.

IV. OTHER BENEFITS

A) Should ARTIST be dismissed from his/her employment by COMPANY, ARTIST shall be paid a sum equal to two (2) weeks regular salary in addition to any salary due at the time of his/her termination with the exception of dismissal for just cause to be determined by Artistic Director and President.

B) ARTIST shall be given the opportunity to reserve two (2) complimentary tickets for each performance series unless sold out. ARTIST shall follow proper procedure as established by the COMPANY for the receipt of said tickets.

V. EQUIPMENT AND SUPPLIES

A) COMPANY agrees to provide the ARTIST with the following equipment and supplies at no expense to ARTIST:

1) All costumes, costume accessories, wigs, hair coloring, and any other make-up other than the ARTIST's normal stage make-up.

a) Said costumes shall be clean at the beginning of each performance period and shall, where practical, be cleaned or laundered after each performance. Reasonable efforts shall be made in order that no ARTIST shall be required to wear an unlaundered garment if required out of necessity to share such garment with another ARTIST. The COMPANY shall make an effort to not have more than two (2) ARTISTS share any costume;

b) Reasonable efforts shall be made to have all costumes in ARTIST's dressing room at least one-half hour prior to curtain.

2) Whenever possible such rehearsal skirts, mock tutus, props and scenic elements as are felt to be of value;

3) COMPANY shall provide performance or rehearsal related shoes for ARTIST. The number of shoes shall not exceed the discretion of the costumer. ARTIST shall be required to complete a shoe and tights contract at the commencement of each contract period.

VI. WORKING CONDITIONS AND STANDARDS

A) COMPANY shall provide the following minimum rehearsal and performance conditions:

1) Floors of rehearsal and performance spaces shall be resilient and non-slippery. ARTIST shall never be required to dance on floors that consist of concrete, wood directly over concrete, marble or tile (except as waived by individual ARTIST). COMPANY shall use reasonable effort to make use of the portable sprung floor in its possession in all performance halls. Final decision shall be at the discretion of the Artistic Director.

2) COMPANY shall use reasonable effort to make all backstage areas safe for the ARTIST; this includes adequate lighting of all crossover passages, and clearly marking all sudden drop offs due to the sprung floor.

3) At all times, temperature in rehearsal hall, studio, performance hall, and dressing rooms shall not be less than sixty-eight (68) degrees Fahrenheit, or exceed ninety (90) degrees Fahrenheit. This required temperature shall be achieved no less than fifteen (15) minutes prior to the scheduled activity.

4) COMPANY shall make reasonable efforts to insure adequate ventilation of all rehearsal and performance spaces.

5) COMPANY shall guarantee the safety of ARTIST to the best of COMPANY's ability. If that ARTIST is required to assume an added risk for performance, such as the use of a trapeze, dance in the area of a flashpot, or dance on a platform, COMPANY shall make reasonable efforts to minimize risk of injury to ARTIST.

6) COMPANY shall make reasonable efforts to provide adequate security in all rehearsal and performance spaces. COMPANY shall also provide a means by which the ARTIST may secure his/her "valuables" during a performance.

B) Reasonable efforts shall be made to ensure that studios, dressing rooms, lounge areas and hallways, over which the COMPANY has control and authority, are maintained with a proper and reasonable degree of cleanliness on a daily basis.

C) All smoking shall be prohibited in all rehearsal and performance spaces, except in designated areas; COMPANY agrees to separate, when possible, smoking ARTISTS from non-smoking ARTISTS in dressing rooms.

VII. REHEARSAL

A) STUDIO—ARTIST may be required to rehearse a maximum of five (5) hours per day on which there are no performances scheduled, Monday through Friday, and three (3) hours only on Saturdays. There shall be a maximum of two (2) hours rehearsal on days on which there is one (1) performance scheduled. Except as provided below, no rehearsals may be scheduled on a day on which there are two (2) performances. Rehearsals in the studio shall be subject to the following regulations:

1) There may be a maximum of three (3) consecutive hours of rehearsal without a break of at least one (1) hour. Each rehearsal hour shall include a break of at least five (5) minutes.

2) Photo calls, costume fittings and other such services shall be counted as rehearsal time and shall be subject to restrictions thereto, unless it is a technical emergency.

3) Tentative rehearsal schedules will be posted by the COMPANY not less than twenty-four (24) hours in advance. Said schedules shall be subject to personnel, facility, and such other exigencies as the Artistic Director may deem appropriate. Costume fittings shall be posted not less than twenty-four (24) hours in advance.

4) Emergency rehearsals and services may be scheduled by the COMPANY for a period of one (1) hour on a two (2) performance day. Emergency rehearsals shall be defined as rehearsals necessitated by illness or injury to an ARTIST, or by technical circumstances which have become known to the COMPANY not more than twenty-four (24) hours in advance or at the discretion of the Artistic Director.

B) PRE-PERFORMANCE REHEARSALS IN THE THEATRE—Total class and rehearsal shall not exceed eight (8) hours on any given day of production week.

C) WHILE ON TOUR—If the company is scheduled for two (2) performances on any given day in a new theatre, there shall be a maximum of two (2) hours spacing rehearsal before the first performance. Dancers will be compensated with overtime for individual spacing time.

VIII. PERFORMANCE

A) There shall be a maximum of two (2) performances scheduled on any day and a maximum of eight (8) performances scheduled in any week.

B) An interval of not less than twelve (12) hours shall be allowed between the end of one day's service and the commencement of the following day's activities as defined by curtain down of one performance to curtain up of the next performance and except as noted in X (d) below.

C) A tentative casting notice shall be posted prior to the fourth rehearsal of each ballet. Notice of understudies shall be posted no later than seven (7) days after the beginning of the rehearsal period. A final casting notice shall be posted no later than one (1) week prior to the opening performance.

D) Visitors are not encouraged in the backstage area and are at no time permitted in the backstage area without the permission of the Stage Manager.

TRAVEL: TOUR WHEN OVERNIGHT STAY REQUIRED

Whenever the ARTIST shall be required to work for the COMPANY outside of the metropolitan Atlanta, Georgia area, the COMPANY shall provide and pay for all Company-related transportation between and within such points outside city of origination. The COMPANY shall also provide and pay for Company-related transportation of a reasonable amount of the ARTIST's personal baggage while outside of Atlanta, Georgia. ARTIST's travel shall be subject to the following restrictions:

A) Whenever the ARTIST shall be required to travel by bus outside the metropolitan Atlanta area, the ARTIST shall have a meal stop of one (1) hour after approximately four (4) hours of travel.

B) On days on which no service is scheduled, travel by bus shall be limited to eight (8) hours. On days on which one (1) performance is scheduled, travel shall be limited to four (4) hours. On days on which two (2) performances are scheduled, no travel shall be permitted. Rest stops, meal stops, and mechanical failure do not count as travel time.

C) Whenever the ARTIST shall be required to travel by air within the continental United States, the total hours of travel shall not exceed ten (10) hours. Air travel time will be calculated from the call for departure from a predetermined gathering point to arrival at final destination, and is to include all waiting time at terminals as well as bus transit at both ends. Airline delay time shall not be counted as travel time.

D) COMPANY agrees that transportation by bus outside the metropolitan Atlanta area shall be first class motor coach, with heating, air conditioning and proper ventilation in working order. Said bus shall also have restroom facilities in working order.

E) All ARTISTS will receive, unless otherwise negotiated, thirty-five dollars ($35.00) a day per diem.

X. Travel: When Overnight Stay Is Not Required

Whenever the ARTIST shall be required to work for the COMPANY outside of the metropolitan Atlanta, Georgia area, and said period of work shall not require an overnight stay, the following restrictions shall apply:

A) COMPANY shall provide and pay for transportation and said transportation shall be by bus and comply with Article IX Section D of the Basic Agreement.

B) The total round trip travel time for such service shall not exceed five (5) hours.

C) ARTIST shall receive a full day's per diem for said day.

D) Twelve (12) hour turn around time shall be counted from the arrival time at the COMPANY's final destination point.

XI. Free Days and Holidays

If it is a non-rehearsal, class or a performance service, i.e. travel, photo call, costume fitting or promotion, a free day will be defined as a twenty-four (24) hour period. In all other cases a free day shall be defined as a full calendar day.

A) The COMPANY shall guarantee the ARTIST one (1) free day within each Monday through Sunday week of employment. Each free day shall occur by not later than seven (7) days following the immediately preceding free day except as provided below:

1) Whenever the ARTIST is on tour outside Atlanta, Georgia for a period of ten (10) days or more, the COMPANY may at its option elect that the span between free days does not exceed ten (10) days.

B) Following any period of touring in excess of seven (7) days, the COMPANY shall use its best efforts to designate the free day on the day immediately following the Company's return to Atlanta, GA.

C) The following holidays shall be designated free days: Labor Day, Thanksgiving Day, Martin Luther King's Birthday, Christmas Eve (after 5:00 p.m.), Christmas Day, New Year's Eve (after 5:00 p.m.), New Year's Day, and Easter Sunday.

D) The COMPANY may, at its discretion, designate two (2) free days following an extended home performance series.

XII. ARTIST'S STANDARDS

During the term of employment, ARTISTS shall be expected to maintain themselves in the physical and technical condition necessary for the performance of their professional duties, and to conduct themselves in a professional manner at all times. At the beginning of the contract period, ARTIST shall present him/herself in physical condition as deemed appropriate for a professional company as determined by the Artistic Director.

XIII. ARTIST'S REPRESENTATIVES

ARTISTS employed by the COMPANY shall appoint or elect two (2) ARTISTS to serve as ARTIST'S representatives.

XIV. EMPLOYMENT CONFERENCE

No later than six (6) weeks prior to the end of the term of employment, ARTIST shall have a conference with the Artistic Director to discuss his/her future employment with the COMPANY.

XV. TALENT RELEASE

Artist agrees to grant The Atlanta Ballet, its agents, and/or their successors, the right to use, publish, or copywrite ARTIST's name, picture, portrait, or likeness in advertising, promotions, or publicity of The Atlanta Ballet in any manner or form, regardless of ARTIST's employment status.

XVI. OUTSIDE ENGAGEMENTS

No ARTIST shall accept assignments, including but not limited to, teaching, performing, and choreographing while committed by signed contract to the COMPANY without the prior written permission of the Artistic Director, notification to the Company Manager and written permission of the President. At any time the ARTIST appears with another organization during the terms of the Agreement, and in accordance within the aforementioned guidelines, program credit must include "Artist appears courtesy of The Atlanta Ballet."

XVII. RESPONSIBILITIES OF ARTIST

1) All ARTISTS shall be in the theatre one-half hour prior to curtain time, regardless of the ARTIST's place on the program. ARTIST shall be required to sign in on sheet provided for that purpose, no later than one-half hour prior to curtain.

2) ARTISTS not in a program are required to make their whereabouts known to the Stage Manager not less than one-half hour prior to curtain.

3) All ARTISTS are to remain for curtain calls.

4) ARTISTS shall not engage in any audible talking, smoking, chewing gum, or any improper conduct either on stage or backstage.

5) No food or drink shall be on stage at any time.

6) ARTISTS shall not stand or sit in the wings where there is a possibility of being seen by any member of the audience, or being a hazard to any other performer.

7) No scenery, electrics or other stage equipment shall be disturbed without permission of the Stage Manager.

8) ARTISTS shall not place any article of clothing on any prop table or on any scenery.

9) ARTISTS shall treat costumes and/or props in a professional manner.

10) ARTISTS shall not drink (other than water), eat, smoke, or sit on the floor in a manner that would abuse a costume, while in costume.

11) ARTIST shall check all of his/her props and costumes in sufficient time prior to a performance and shall notify proper personnel of any problem.

12) ARTISTS shall not wear any jewelry on stage, unless it is required or has been approved by the Artistic Director or his designate.

13) ARTISTS shall not change any choreography without the prior approval of the Artistic Director or his designate.

14) ARTISTS shall be expected to participate in photo calls, press events, and special events from time to time as determined by the Artistic Director and President in order to assist in the promotion and development activities of the COMPANY.

XVIII. FINES

A) ARTIST agrees that the COMPANY shall have the right to fine an individual ARTIST $10.00 after two (2) written warnings, for the offenses listed below. All fines and penalties are under the discretion of the Artistic Staff in conjunction with the Company Manager.

1) ARTIST being late, or missing any rehearsal, costume fitting, or photo call without prior notification to Artistic Director and Company Manager.

2) ARTIST causing delay in scheduled departure time of COMPANY provided transportation.

3) ARTIST keeping the curtain waiting without legitimate excuse.

4) Unprofessional behavior of ARTIST on stage or in the backstage area.

5) Unprofessional behavior of ARTIST towards the Artistic Staff or his/her fellow ARTISTS during any official COMPANY function.

6) The wearing of personal or street jewelry on stage that is not part of a costume or without receiving prior approval of the Artistic Director or his designate.

7) A female ARTIST's hair becoming unpinned or pointe shoe ribbon becoming untied during a performance.

8) Smoking in a non-designated smoking area.

B) ARTIST agrees that the COMPANY shall have the right to fine an individual ARTIST without warning for the offenses listed below. Appropriate fine for said offense appears after each section.

1) ARTIST being late for a performance. FINE: $1/5$th of the ARTIST's weekly pay.

2) ARTIST missing an entrance without legitimate excuse. FINE: $25.00

3) ARTIST missing a curtain call without legitimate excuse. FINE: $25.00

4) ARTIST changing any choreography, other than for such reasons as honestly and obviously forgetting choreography, compensating for another ARTIST who has forgotten choreography, or compensating for some unavoidable accident or situation over which the ARTIST has no control. FINE: $1/5$th of the ARTIST's weekly pay.

5) ARTIST damaging a costume due to negligence or carelessness of ARTIST while said costume is in ARTIST's control, such as food stains, cigarette burns, etc. Should such damage occur, ARTIST shall pay for cost of cleaning costume, repair of costume, or cost of replacing costume if necessary due to extent of damage.

6) ARTIST failing to appear for a performance, without legitimate excuse, or prior written approval of Artistic Director, shall be fined $1/2$ of his/her weekly salary and may be grounds for dismissal.

XIX. Overtime Compensation

Whenever the ARTIST shall be required by the COMPANY to perform any service over the maximum allowable number of hours as stated in this Agreement, ARTIST shall be compensated at the rate of $12.50 per one-half hour, or any part thereof, after a grace period of five (5) minutes.

A) In the case of travel, overtime caused by mechanical failure or circumstances beyond the control of the COMPANY shall be excluded from overtime compensation.

B) Whenever the ARTIST shall be required by the COMPANY to perform any service beyond the maximum number of allowable days without a free day as stated in this Agreement, the ARTIST shall be compensated with ⅙th of his/her weekly pay.

XX. Rights of Management

In recognition of the flexibility needed by The Atlanta Ballet, Inc. to achieve the purposes of this Agreement, The Atlanta Ballet, Inc. and the Dancers of The Atlanta Ballet, Inc. hereby agree that the COMPANY shall have the right to issue reasonable rules and regulations from time to time that do not conflict with the expressed terms of this Agreement.

XXI. Legal Jurisdiction

This Agreement shall be interpreted in accordance with the Laws of the State of Georgia.

XXII. Disagreement Resolution

If, from time to time, disagreements arise as to the meaning of a term or provision, or an application of a provision, the parties agree to enter into a joint discussion to seek a reasonable solution.

If no reasonable solution can be achieved, the parties hereby agree that the disagreement shall be submitted to a committee of no less than three (3) nor more than five (5) persons appointed by the Chairman of the Board. The decision of such committee shall be final and binding upon both parties for the duration of this Agreement.

THIS AGREEMENT CONSTITUTES THE ENTIRE AGREEMENT BETWEEN ARTIST AND COMPANY AND SHALL BE BINDING FOR CONTRACT PERIOD ONLY AS DEFINED ABOVE.

Sample Photo Release Form

I (we), the undersigned, hereby waive and release all rights we may have regarding ownership or use of photographs bearing my (our) image taken for purposes of public relations for the _____ Ballet Co., and grant permission to said company to use and display said photographs for commercial or noncommercial use for said company including film, video tape or still production.

_____   /s/_____
Date   Dancer

_____   /s/_____
Date   Witness

Glossary of Common Theatre Terms

BACKDROP	A hanging, painted piece of scenery.
BOOM	A vertical pipe for mounting lights.
BOOTH	The room from which lighting technicians work the lights.
CATWALKS	System of narrow bridges above the stage and audience.
COVES	Areas to hang lights above the audience.
CREW	The men and women who work backstage.
CROSSOVER	Space behind backdrop allowing dancers to cross from one side of the stage to the other out of view of the audience.
CUE	A predetermined signal to make an entrance onto the stage.
CYC	Short for cyclorama, a plain backdrop that can be lit in many ways.
DIMMER	Apparatus for altering the flow of electricity, causing the lights to be more or less bright.
DOWNSTAGE	The area of the stage nearest to the audience.
DRESSER	A person who helps the dancers get into costume.
ELECTRICS	The pipes holding the lights above the stage.
FLY IN OR OUT	To lower or raise set pieces or drops.
FLY SYSTEM	The system designed to raise and lower the sets and drops.
FRESNEL	A stage light recognized by its concentric rings on the lens.
GRAND DRAPE	Main curtain of the proscenium, designed to tie in with the house decor. Separates the stage from the audience. Also called the house or act curtain.
GREEN ROOM	A waiting area close to the stage area. Usually used by musicians and/or the conductor and for small after-performance receptions.

GRID	The iron walkways above the stage.
"HEADS"	The call given by stage crew when equipment is being lowered from the flys.
HOUSE	The part of the theatre in which the audience sits.
LAMP	The correct name for the bulb used in stage lights.
LEGS	The curtains hanging at the side of the stage that create wings.
LEIKO	An ellipsoidal reflector spotlight.
MARLEY	A pliable linoleum commonly called a dance floor.
OFFSTAGE	Out of sight of the audience away from the center of the stage.
ONSTAGE	In sight of the audience. Toward the center of the stage.
"PLACES (PLEASE)!"	The command given by the stage manager calling all artists to the stage five minutes prior to curtain time.
PRODUCTION MANAGER	The person who oversees the production (see chap. 3).
PROMPT CORNER	The downstage corner used by the stage manager to call the show. Originally the corner used by the prompter.
PROSCENIUM	The arch or frame in front of the grand drape and between the audience and stage.
QUICK-CHANGE ROOM	A small room very close to the stage area used for fast changes during the performance.
RAKED STAGE	Floor angled toward the footlights and audience.
RIGGING	The ropes or heavy wires used to lower or raise the scenery.
ROAD BOXES	Wooden boxes on wheels that are used to transport costumes, scenery, or electrical equipment.
SCENE SHOP	Area where scenery is built and/or stored.
SCRIM	A curtain with a weave that allows the dancer, standing behind it, to be seen when lit from behind, but not when the light is projected on the front of it.
SPOTLIGHT	Term used for the single light that follows a star or principal character (the best place to be!).
STAGE DOOR	The door at the back or side of the theatre that leads to the backstage area.
STAGE LEFT	To the dancer's left as he or she faces the audience.
STAGE RIGHT	To the dancer's right as he or she faces the audience.
STRIKE	The process of dismantling the scenery, sets, lights, and costumes and packing them into the trucks for transportation.
TECHY OR GRIP	Stagehand.

THEATRE CASES	The suitcases allocated each dancer to transport makeup, etc. These travel with the costumes and sets in the trucks.
TRAPS	System of openings through the stage floor.
TREES	Metal posts that hold lighting instruments, usually in the wings.
UPSTAGE	The area farthest away from the audience.
WARDROBE	The room where all costumes are constructed and stored. Also loose term for the costume department.
WINGS	The spaces at each side of the stage where the dancer awaits a cue.

Bibliography

Ashley, Merrill. *Dancing for Balanchine*. New York: E. P. Dutton, 1984.

Berthold, Margot. *History of World Theatre*. New York: Fredrick Ungar, 1972.

Chujoy, Anatole, and P. W. Manchester, eds. *The Dance Encyclopedia*. New York: Simon and Schuster, 1967.

Danilova, Alexandra. *Choura*. New York: Knopf, 1986.

de Mille, Agnes. *Dance to the Piper*. Boston: Little, Brown, 1951.

Ellis, Havelock. *Dance as Life*. New York: Houghton Mifflin, 1923.

Fonteyn, Margot. *Autobiography*. London: W. H. Allen, 1972.

———. *The Magic of Dance*. New York: Knopf, 1979.

Geva, Tamara. *Split Seconds*. New York: Harper and Row, 1972.

Gordon, Suzanne. *Off Balance*. New York: Pantheon Books, 1983.

Grigoriev, S. L. *The Diaghilev Ballet 1909–1929*. Penguin Books, London, 1953.

Guest, Ivor, Richard Buckle, Barry Kay, and Liz daCosta. *Designing for Dancers*. New York: Universe Publishing, 1981.

Hrosko, Mariane. *Dancer's Survival Book*. New York: Harper and Row, 1987.

Kent, Allegra. *The Dancer's Body Book*. New York: Quill, 1984.

Neilson, Eric Brandt. *Dance Auditions*. Princeton, N.J.: Princeton Books, 1984.

Parker, W. Oreon, and Harvey K. Smith. *Scene Design and Stage Lighting*. New York: Holt, Rinehart, and Winston, 1970.

Payne, Charles. *American Ballet Theatre*. New York: Knopf, 1978.

Rambert, Marie. *Quicksilver*. London: Macmillan, 1972.

Ryan, Allan J., and Robert E. Stephens. *A Dancer's Guide to Health-Care and a Long Career*. Princeton, N.J.: Princeton Books, 1987.

Sammarco, G. James. *Sports Medicine*. Philadelphia: W. B. Saunders Co., 1983.

Shaller, Ludmilla, and Anatole Vilzak. *A Ballerina Prepares*. Princeton, N.J.: Princeton Books, 1982.

Vincent, L. M. *Competing with the Sylph*. Princeton, N.J.: Princeton Books, 1989.

———. *The Dancer's Book of Health*. Princeton, N.J.: Princeton Books, 1988.

Whitehill, Angela, and William Noble. *The Parent's Book of Ballet*. Colorado Springs, Co.: Meriwether Publishing, Ltd., 1988.